Great American Writers

TWENTIETH CENTURY

EDITOR

R. BAIRD SHUMAN

University of Illinois

Jack London • Archibald MacLeish

Bernard Malamud • David Mamet • Edgar Lee Masters

Cormac McCarthy • Carson McCullers • D'Arcy McNickle

MARSHALL CAVENDISH

NEW YORK • TORONTO • LONDON • SYDNEY

Marshall Cavendish
99 White Plains Road
Tarrytown, New York 10591-9001

Website: www.marshallcavendish.com

Salem Press

    Editor: R. Baird Shuman
    Managing Editor: R. Kent Rasmussen

    Manuscript Editors: Heather Stratton
                       Lauren M. Mitchell
    Assistant Editor: Andrea Miller
    Research Supervisor: Jeffry Jensen
    Acquisitions Editor: Mark Rehn

Marshall Cavendish

    Project Editor: Marian Armstrong
    Editorial Director: Paul Bernabeo

Designer: Patrice Sheridan

Photo Research: Candlepants
                Carousel Research
                Linda Sykes Picture Research
                Anne Burns Images

Indexing: AEIOU

Library of Congress Cataloging-in-Publication Data

Great American writers: twentieth century / R. Baird Shuman, editor.
    v. cm.
    Includes bibliographical references and indexes.
    Contents: v. 1. Agee-Bellow--v. 2. Benét-Cather--v. 3. Cormier-
Dylan--v. 4. Eliot-Frost--v. 5. Gaines-Hinton--v. 6. Hughes-Lewis--v. 7.
London-McNickle--v. 8. Miller-O'Connor--v. 9. O'Neill-Rich--v. 10.
Salinger-Stein--v. 11. Steinbeck-Walker--v. 12. Welty-Zindel--v. 13.
Index.
    ISBN 0-7614-7240-1 (set)—ISBN 0-7614-7247-9 (v. 7)
    1. American literature--20th century--Bio-bibliography--
Dictionaries. 2. Authors, American--20th century--Biography--
Dictionaries. 3. American literature--20th century--Dictionaries. I.
Shuman, R. Baird (Robert Baird), 1929-

PS221.G74 2002
810.9'005'03
[B]   2001028461

Printed in Malaysia; bound in the United States

07 06 05 04 03 02   6 5 4 3 2 1

Contents

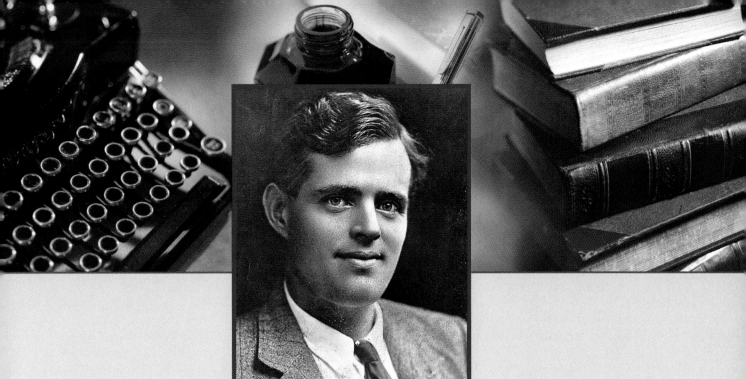

Jack London

BORN: January 12, 1876, San Francisco, California
DIED: November 22, 1916, Glen Ellen, California
IDENTIFICATION: Prolific early twentieth-century novelist and short-story writer who gained critical and popular success with his realistic tales of adventure and hardship in Canada and Alaska.

Jack London wrote his most successful works at a time when sentimental fiction dominated the American literary market. In works such as *The Call of the Wild* (1903), *White Fang* (1906), and *The Sea-Wolf* (1904), he explored the primitive roots of modern life and captured the imagination of a readership that was drawn to the realistic adventures and exotic settings of his stories. London's works have been embraced by readers throughout the world, and complete editions of his writings have been published in France, Germany, and Russia. Most of his books remain in print in multiple editions and are featured regularly in high school and university curricula.

The Writer's Life

Jack London was born John Griffith Chaney on January 12, 1876, in a working-class neighborhood in San Francisco, California. His presumed father, William Chaney, gave lectures on astrology, and his mother, Flora Wellman, was a spiritualist and music teacher. London's mother came from a prosperous Midwest family. At sixteen, she made her way to California, where she met Chaney, a self-described professor of astrology. Although they never married, the two lived and worked together, giving lectures on astrology and spiritualism in and around San Francisco. According to Flora, when she became pregnant, Chaney threatened to leave her if she did not terminate the pregnancy. She refused, making two suicide attempts that were publicized in local newspapers. Chaney fled to Oregon, leaving Flora to depend on the charity of neighbors and friends.

Surrogate Father. Eight months after the birth of her son, Flora married John London, a Civil War veteran, who adopted young John Chaney and gave him the name that would become famous in later years, Jack London. In addition to a new father, London now had two stepsisters, Eliza and Ida, John London's children from a previous marriage. Because Flora was often too busy to take care of her young son, Eliza took responsibility for him, providing the attention he did not receive from his mother. London also had a nurse, an African American woman named Virginia Prentiss, called Mammy Jennie, who treated him as one of her own children.

An Early Wanderer. When London and Eliza came down with a near-fatal case of diphtheria, their father moved the family across the San Francisco Bay to Oakland and opened a grocery store. The family prospered for a time, until the store failed. During the mid-1880s, the London family moved several times: to a twenty-acre farm in Alameda, to a seventy-five-acre pasture on the coast of San Mateo County, and to a small ranch in the Livermore Valley. John London tried to become an independent farmer, mortgaging the new ranch heavily to pay for equip-

Jack London had very little formal education due to his family's frequent relocations and the need for him to earn money. Always an insatiable reader, he was largely self-taught. An adventurer with a wide variety of experiences and acquaintances, he had much to tell.

ment and outbuildings. In 1886, after losing the ranch, the family returned to an eight-room home in Oakland, which they used as a boarding house.

Education. Jack London's formal education was brief and sporadic. He graduated from the Cole School in Oakland in 1891. Instead of entering high school, he worked to support his family. At nineteen, he returned to school, attending Oakland High for one year; however, the slow pace of his classes and a growing boredom compelled him to quit. After five weeks in an accelerated program to prepare for college entrance examinations, he withdrew to study on his own nineteen hours a day for three months. He passed his exams and enrolled at the University of California at Berkeley, where he completed one semester before abandoning formal education for good.

From an early age, London was a voracious reader. After he settled in Oakland, he discovered the public library and began checking out books regularly. He read widely, relying on the assistance of the head librarian, Ina Coolbrith, to help direct his reading.

As a boy, London routinely held many odd jobs. At fifteen, he began working ten-hour days at a cannery for ten cents an hour. He would later make a lot more by raiding the oyster beds of San Francisco Bay where he was dubbed Prince of the Oyster Pirates. Eventually he would become the highest paid and best-selling writer of his age.

The Oakland Waterfront. While still in grammar school, London managed two newspaper routes, set pins in a bowling alley, and worked on an ice truck to help support his family. As his stepfather's health declined and as Flora routinely mismanaged the family's meager financial resources, London began work at a cannery in 1891 for ten cents an hour, rarely working fewer than ten hours a day. After more than a year of grinding labor and handing most of his earnings over to his mother, London left the cannery. He purchased a small skiff with the money he had saved and spent all his spare time on the waters of San Francisco Bay.

At fifteen, London joined the riffraff that inhabited the Oakland waterfront. With a loan from Mammy Jennie, he purchased a sloop called the *Razzle Dazzle*. He began raiding the oyster beds along the bay at night and selling the spoils to waterfront eateries in the morning. In a single evening, he earned more by stealing oysters than he did in several months in the cannery. The waterfront community dubbed him the Prince of the Oyster Pirates for his reckless bravery on the water and his ability to hold his liquor on land.

Life on the bay was precarious, and many fell prey to the violent competition among the oyster pirates or the dangers of alcohol abuse. London, who had lived and worked among the pirates, as well as the local Fish Patrol, escaped the dangers of the bay and signed on with the *Sophia Sutherland*, a sealing schooner that

To escape the dangers of the waterfront, London signed on with a schooner bound for Japan. He immediately took to life on the sea and, years later, would build the *Snark*, on which he hoped but failed to sail around the world. Seen here is W. Herbert Dunton's painting *With Jack London Aboard the* Snark—*Christmas Morning in Mid-Ocean*.

sailed for Japan. With only the experience of a small-boat sailor, he quickly adapted to life on the open sea, steering the ship through stormy oceans and holding his own in the saloons of the Bonin Islands.

First Literary Success.

When London returned to Oakland after three months at sea, he submitted a story to a writing competition held by the *San Francisco Morning Call*. His "Story of a Typhoon off the Coast of Japan" took first prize and was published in the newspaper. London received twenty-five dollars and began to consider writing as a possible career.

Road Life and Gold Fever.

After working briefly in a jute mill and an electrical plant shoveling coal for the same wage he had earned as a boy in the cannery, London joined "Kelly's Army," a large band of unemployed workers marching on Washington, D.C., to protest economic conditions. He abandoned the march in Kansas City, Missouri, and hopped freight trains across the eastern United States. He was arrested at Niagara Falls for vagrancy and served thirty days in jail. In 1897 he accompanied his brother-in-law to the Yukon in search of gold. Although he found none and suffered a severe case of scurvy, he did find the material for his most enduring works of fiction.

The Writing Game.

Upon his return from the Yukon, London discovered that his stepfather had died and his mother was in debt and struggling to pay off her creditors. He looked for work, even taking civil service exams for postal work. He also settled down to a rigid discipline of study and writing. After hundreds of rejection letters and several trips to the pawn shop, he published "To the Man on the Trail" in the *Overland Monthly* in 1899. A year later, "An Odyssey of the North" appeared in the *Atlantic Monthly*, and London became a professional writer.

Married Life and Success.

Flushed by his recent success, London married Bess Maddern, the fiancé of a friend who had recently died. The marriage was more about business than love. London seemed to want the stability that married life would provide as he devoted more time to his writing. He also wanted children, and his first child, Joan, was born in 1901. She was followed by a second daughter, Becky, in 1902.

London spent the summer of 1902 in the East End slums of London, England, observing conditions among the homeless and working poor. He published his experiences there in *The People of the Abyss* (1903) and became a spokesman for numerous leftist causes. In 1903 he published *The Call of the Wild*, which became an instant classic, followed in 1904 by *The Sea-Wolf*, also a best-seller. London's writing career was flourishing. His marriage, however, had all but crumbled. He left for Korea and Japan in 1904 to cover the Russo-Japanese War for William Randolph Hearst's newspapers. Upon his return, Bess had already begun divorce proceedings.

London had two daughters, Joan and Becky, with his first wife, Bess Maddern. His second wife Charmian Kittredge and he were not as fortunate.

HIGHLIGHTS IN LONDON'S LIFE

1876   Jack London is born John Griffith Chaney on January 12 in San Francisco, California; is adopted by John London eight months later.

1880   His family moves to Oakland.

1886   London meets a librarian, Ina Coolbrith, who helps direct his reading.

1891   Graduates from grammar school; begins work in a cannery; becomes an oyster pirate on San Francisco Bay; later joins the Fish Patrol.

1893   Sails to the Far East on a sealing ship; wins first prize in newspaper essay contest.

1894   Joins the unemployed Kelly's Army to march on Washington, D.C.; is arrested in Niagara Falls for vagrancy.

1895   Attends Oakland High School.

1896   Joins the Socialist Labor Party; attends the University of California at Berkeley.

1897   Joins the Klondike gold rush.

1898   Contracts scurvy and returns to Oakland.

1899   Publishes first professional story and begins writing for a living.

1900   Marries Bess Maddern; publishes his first collection of stories, *The Son of the Wolf.*

1901   First daughter, Joan, is born.

1902   London spends six weeks in London's East End; second daughter, Becky, is born; London publishes first novel, *A Daughter of the Snows.*

1903   Publishes *The Call of the Wild*, an instant success.

1904   Serves as war correspondent during the Russo-Japanese War.

1905   Is divorced by Bess; marries Charmian Kittredge; purchases ranch near Glen Ellen, California.

1906   Begins building the *Snark* for sailing voyage around the world.

1907   Leaves on world tour aboard the *Snark*; visits Hawaii, the Marquesas, and Tahiti.

1909   Is hospitalized in Australia; abandons voyage and returns to California.

1910   Begins building Wolf House.

1913   Wolf House burns to the ground.

1914   London reports on the Mexican Revolution for *Collier's.*

1915   Returns to Hawaii for health reasons; is warned by doctor to curb his drinking and eating habits.

1916   Resigns from the Socialist Party; dies of uremic poisoning on November 22 in Glen Ellen.

Beauty Ranch and Wolf House. Prior to his divorce from Bess, London had purchased a small ranch on 130 acres of land in Sonoma County, just north of San Francisco Bay. He eventually built the ranch up to 1,400 acres. The day after his divorce was final, he married Charmian Kittredge and settled at what he called Beauty Ranch. He also began building the *Snark,* a boat on which he planned a seven-year trip around the world with his new wife. Though he did sail to the South Pacific and Australia, he spent only two years aboard the *Snark;* he contracted a series of tropical viruses that forced him to cut short his trip. After a stop in Australia for medical treatment, he and Charmian returned to Beauty Ranch.

In 1910 London saw construction begin on a grand estate, which he called Wolf House. Immense in proportion and built from local materials, the house was nearly complete in 1913, with a price tag of more than seventy thousand dollars. On the night of August 21, 1913, Wolf House burned to the ground. Arson was suspected but could not be proved. In 1914 London went to Mexico to report on the Mexican Revolution for *Collier's.*

Decline. Following the destruction of Wolf House, mounting financial pressures, the death of a child with Charmian at birth, and later a miscarriage, London fell into a deep depression. His health had been generally poor since his voyage on the *Snark,* and his drinking, with which he had struggled for years, was affecting his kidneys. He sought to improve his health by traveling briefly to Hawaii in 1915. He continued to write and devoted much of his dwindling energy in plans to improve Beauty Ranch. On the night of November 21, 1916, London took morphine to ease his almost-constant pain. The next day, he slipped into a coma and died. Some biographers have suggested that London committed suicide; however, scholars agree that the cause of death was uremic poisoning.

FILMS BASED ON LONDON'S STORIES

1908 *For Love of Gold*

1908 *The Call of the Wild*

1913 *The Sea-Wolf*

1914 *The Valley of the Moon*

1914 *John Barleycorn*

1914 *The Chechako*

1914 *Burning Daylight: The Adventures of Burning Daylight in Civilization*

1914 *Martin Eden*

1914 *An Odyssey of the North*

1920 *The Star Rover*

1920 *The Sea-Wolf*

1922 *The Son of the Wolf*

1925 *Adventure*

1925 *White Fang*

1928 *Tropical Nights*

1936 *Conflict*

1940 *Queen of the Yukon*

1941 *The Sea-Wolf*

1950 *Barricade*

1952 *The Fighter*

1969 *The Assassination Bureau*

1980 *Klondike Fever*

1991 *White Fang*

1997 *The Sea-Wolf*

The Writer's Work

Jack London was a disciplined and prolific writer, publishing over fifty books between 1899 and 1916. They included novels, short stories, plays, essays, sociological studies, and children's fiction. He is best known, however, for his short fiction, particularly his stories and short novels set in Alaska and the Klondike region of Canada during the gold rush era. His ability to portray life as he experienced it gave his work a vitality that appealed to a wide range of audiences.

London's first of over fifty published works was called "Story of a Typhoon off the Coast of Japan." Based on his exploits aboard a sealing vessel, it took first prize in a local writing competition and appeared in the *San Francisco Morning Call*.

Issues in London's Fiction. Many of London's characters possess a sense of their ancestral roots. In *The Call of the Wild*, for example, the dog Buck dreams of an older age, when he sat by the fire of a primitive man. Ultimately, he discovers his kinship with the wolf and obeys his instinct to return to the wilderness. The narrator of *Before Adam* (1906) describes the life he led during an early stage of human evolution. These so-called racial memories provide a link between humanity's modern present and primordial past.

London studied Charles Darwin's theory of evolution, particularly the British sociologist Herbert Spencer's commentaries on Darwin. He witnessed men and women struggling for survival against a harsh natural environment during his days in the Yukon, and he experienced the brutality of human beings during his days on the Oakland waterfront and as a hobo riding the trains. He saw that the strong survive, the weak perish, and the natural world remains unaffected by either. Characters in London's fiction are continually forced to adapt to their environment and to understand and respect their limitations or risk destruction.

People in London's Fiction.

London created a wide variety of characters, presenting his readers with portraits that were previously unknown or seldom seen in American literature. In *The Road* (1907), for example, he examines the tramp life of hobos riding the rails and describes the language and culture of this obscure and persecuted community. In *The Iron Heel* (1907), his character Ernest Everhart embodies many of his own socialist views.

Among the most enduring characters in London's fiction are his animal heroes, such as Buck of *The Call of the Wild* and the title character of *White Fang*. Both animals preserve their inner natures against staggering physical and environmental hardships. London's memorable human characters include Wolf Larsen, the sadistic captain in *The Sea-Wolf*, and Martin Eden, whose relentless pursuit of a writing career mirrors London's own efforts to become an author.

The White Logic. In one of his autobiographical works, *John Barleycorn* (1913), London examines a form of reasoning that he calls "white logic," which comes to him while under the influence of alcohol. "John Barleycorn sends his White Logic, the argent messenger of truth beyond truth, the antithesis of life, cruel and bleak as interstellar space, pulseless and frozen as absolute zero, dazzling with the frost of irrefragable logic and unforgettable fact." Conventional logic suggests that the struggle for survival is a worthwhile one and that life has meaning and purpose. White logic, in contrast, removes these illusions and reveals the impermanence of all things and the ambivalence of the world toward all human striving.

In many of his other works, London develops the idea of white logic in a different context, apart from the nature and abuse of alcohol. When London's characters confront the Yukon's frozen wilderness, in stories such as "To Build a Fire" and "The White Silence," they face a form of the white logic. When Martin Eden sees the futility of his own existence, London writes that "his danger lay in that he was not afraid. If he were only afraid, he would make toward life." This, too, is the white logic, for, as London states further in *John Barleycorn*, "the world-sickness of the White Logic makes one grin jocosely into the face of the Noseless One [death] and to sneer at all the phantasmagoria of living."

London's Literary Legacy. During his lifetime, London was the highest paid and best-

SOME INSPIRATIONS BEHIND LONDON'S WORK

Jack London's early exposure to literature, particularly the works of Rudyard Kipling, the travel books of Paul du Chaillu, and Ouida's *Signa* (1875), gave him a thirst for adventure and travel as well as a belief that one could rise above one's surroundings. London's own adventures became a source for his writing. His days as an oyster pirate on San Francisco Bay and as a hobo riding freight trains, his experiences in the Klondike during the gold rush, and his service on the *Sophia Sutherland* all gave him raw material for his most enduring fictions. His contact with a wide variety of social and economic classes, moreover, provided the inspiration for his numerous sociological studies, including *The People of the Abyss* (1903) and his socialist essays.

While London's real-life adventures provided a framework for his fictional adventure stories, his prolific reading in philosophy and the social sciences provided their substance. Darwin's *On the Origin of Species* (1859) played an important role in shaping the relationships of London's fictional characters, particularly through Herbert Spencer's interpretations of Darwin's theories.

London describes the impact of Spencer's thought on his own life in the semiautobiographical novel *Martin Eden* (1908). Other influences include the German philosopher Friedrich Nietzsche, the German naturalist Ernst Haeckel, and the German socialist theorist Karl Marx, who provided the substance for London's own socialist beliefs.

London settled with Charmian on a 1400-acre ranch north of San Francisco Bay. Here they built an estate that burned to the ground when nearly complete. Luck was also against them aboard the *Snark*. What had been planned as a seven-year journey was cut to two years owing to a series of tropical viruses Jack contracted in the South Pacific and Australia.

selling writer in the United States. His works inspired many of the next generation of American writers, including Upton Sinclair and Ernest Hemingway. The hardships of London's upbringing among San Francisco's working-class poor and his travels through many parts of the world inspired a passionate regard for the underprivileged that is conveyed most notably in his social writings.

Although critics often cite London's difficulty in sustaining the organization and quality of his longer narratives as well as his consistently unrealistic portrayal of female characters, they also recognize his mastery of the short story form. In many ways distinctively American, London's work has been embraced by many countries and age groups. His ability to infuse simple tales with his own complex philosophical spec-

ulations creates multiple layers of meaning in his work that continue to challenge and fascinate modern scholars and readers.

BIBLIOGRAPHY

Cassuto, Leonard, and Jeanne Campbell Reesman, eds. *Rereading Jack London*. Stanford, Calif.: Stanford University Press, 1996.

Dyer, Daniel. *Jack London: A Biography*. New York: Scholastic Trade, 1997.

Hedrick, Joan. *Solitary Comrade: Jack London and His Work*. Chapel Hill: University of North Carolina Press, 1982.

Kershaw, Alex. *Jack London: A Life*. New York: St. Martin's Press, 1997.

Labor, Earle, and Jeanne Campbell Reesman. *Jack London*. Rev. ed. New York: Twayne Publishers, 1994.

Lewis, Sinclair. *Jack: A Biography of Jack London*. New York: Harper and Row, 1977.

Shepherd, Irving, and King Hendricks. *Letters from Jack London*. New York: Odyssey Press, 1965.

Tavernier-Courbin, Jacqueline, ed. *Critical Essays on Jack London*. Boston: G. K. Hall, 1983.

Walker, Dale L., and Jeanne Campbell Reesman. *No Mentor but Myself: Jack London on Writing and Writers*. Stanford, Calif.: Stanford University Press, 1999.

Walker, Franklin. *Jack London and the Klondike*. San Marino, Calif.: Huntington Library Press, 1994.

SHORT FICTION

1900 The Son of the Wolf
1901 The God of His Fathers and Other Stories
1902 Children of the Frost
1904 The Faith of Men and Other Stories
1906 Moon-Face and Other Stories
1906 Love of Life and Other Stories
1910 Lost Face
1911 When God Laughs and Other Stories
1911 South Sea Tales
1912 The House of Pride and Other Tales of Hawaii
1912 Smoke Bellew Tales
1912 A Son of the Sun
1913 The Night-Born
1914 The Strength of the Strong
1916 The Turtles of Tasman
1917 The Human Drift
1918 The Red One
1919 On the Makaloa Mat
1922 Dutch Courage and Other Stories

PLAYS

1906 Scorn of Women
1910 Theft
1916 The Acorn-Planter

CHILDREN'S LITERATURE

1902 The Cruise of the Dazzler
1905 Tales of the Fish Patrol

LONG FICTION

1902 A Daughter of the Snows
1903 The Call of the Wild
1904 The Sea-Wolf
1905 The Game
1906 White Fang
1906 Before Adam
1907 The Iron Heel
1908 Martin Eden
1910 Burning Daylight
1911 Adventure
1913 The Abysmal Brute
1913 The Valley of the Moon
1914 The Mutiny of the Elsinore
1915 The Scarlet Plague
1915 The Star Rover
1916 The Little Lady of the Big House
1917 Jerry of the Islands
1917 Michael, Brother of Jerry
1920 Hearts of Three
1963 The Assassination Bureau, Ltd. (completed by Robert L. Fish)

NONFICTION

1903 The Kempton-Wace Letters (with Anna Strunsky)
1903 The People of the Abyss
1905 The War of the Classes
1907 The Road
1910 Revolution and Other Essays
1911 The Cruise of the Snark
1913 John Barleycorn
1965 Letters from Jack London, ed. King Hendricks and Irving Shepard

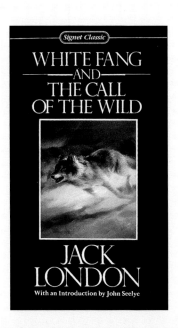

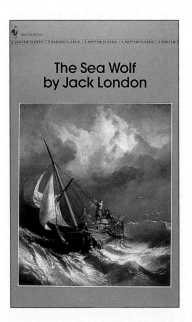

Jack London in London's East End

By 1902 Jack London had finished his first novel, *Daughter of the Snows* (1902), three volumes of short stories, and the children's adventure story *The Cruise of the Dazzler* (1902). His literary reputation was growing, primarily because of his Klondike stories. However, London sympathized with the underprivileged, working-class people who struggled to survive within an economic system that seemed to favor the upper classes. As a high school student, London had published essays on socialism in his school newspaper and earned the nickname Boy Socialist. He felt that he had more to offer in his writing than adventure stories.

The Assignment. In July 1902 London accepted an assignment with the American Press Association to report on the peace process in South Africa following the Boer War. He prepared to sail for England, but the assignment was subsequently canceled. He traveled instead to New York to meet with George Brett, his publisher at Macmillan and Company. Brett suggested the idea of a sociological study of the East End slums in London, England, as the topic of London's next book. London agreed and sailed for England.

Into the Abyss. Upon his arrival, London assumed the role of a down-and-out American sailor stranded in England. He purchased suitable clothing from a secondhand shop, found a room at the home of a private investigator where he could write and clean up when necessary, and then plunged into the dirt and misery of England's most economically depressed and socially degraded urban area.

In the preface to his study of life in London's East End, *People of the Abyss* (1903), London states his criteria for evaluating life in the East End: "That which made for more life, for physical and spiritual health, was good; that which made for less life, which hurt, and dwarfed, and distorted life, was bad." In the crowded boardinghouses where families packed themselves into poorly ventilated and unsanitary rooms and along the streets where the homeless were forced to walk all night because sleeping in the streets after dark was forbidden, London found much that was bad. He sought out the worst areas

Jack London was a lifelong reader of books. From travel journals to the works of Rudyard Kipling, they provided the means of escape from a difficult boyhood. Later, books on philosophy, social science, on Charles Darwin, and Karl Marx would help shape his own thought.

Once nicknamed Boy Socialist, London had a passionate regard for people similar to those on the canvas of Everett Shinn's 1904 painting *Eviction (Lower East Side)* (Smithsonian American Art Museum, Washington, D. C.). He worked with them in his youth, he met them hopping freight trains, and he lived with them in a London slum while researching a sociological study.

of the East End, examined the social institutions that were designed to provide relief for the needy, and interviewed the people who suffered daily from disease and malnutrition.

The People. Among the field laborers, sailors, industrial workers, and homeless of the slums, London found people who had once made comfortable livings and had been able to support their families. Some had even served their country with great distinction. While waiting in line at the casual ward, a government institution that provided temporary beds and meals for the homeless, London met a military hero, a recipient of the Victoria Cross, who by then was an old man wandering the streets of the East End. With compassion and outrage, London described how intelligent and virile people had been reduced to a state of brutish poverty because the value of their labor had been reduced to nothing.

The Problem. Mismanagement, according to London, created the conditions under which so many of England's working poor had to struggle to survive. He believed that with the country's great wealth, no citizen of the British Empire should starve; none should want for employment; and the injured, the aged, and the unfortunate should be cared for by compassionate and efficient social institutions.

London's poignant, eyewitness description of the coronation of King Edward VII captures the irony of life in the East End. While King Edward rode his magnificent carriage through the streets of London, surrounded by the conquered people of England's vast empire and dressed in the richest finery, the unfortunates of the East End were eating rotten orange peels picked from the filthy streets and stealing moments of sleep when the police were not looking.

Conclusions. Of *The People of the Abyss*, London remarked that "no other book of mine took so much of my young heart and tears as that study of the economic degradation of the poor." As a sociological treatise, the book suffers from an emotionally unrestrained response to conditions in the East End. Some critics have even accused London of opportunism, analyzing the conditions he witnessed on the basis of his own socialist preconceptions rather than direct observation. However, he had an ability to convey the hopelessness of the poor in vivid detail and to illustrate the increasing gap between the wealth of the few and the squalor of the many.

London's criticisms of economic conditions among the working classes in England in *The People of the Abyss* appear in different forms in such later works as *The War of the Classes* (1905), *The Road* (1907), *The Iron Heel* (1907), and *Martin Eden* (1908). In particular, his critique of capitalism's mismanagement of economic resources provides the impetus for the attempted socialist revolution in *The Iron Heel*. London's passionate allegiance to the labor classes never wavered during his lifetime, and he used every opportunity in his writing to address the issue of economic oppression, whether in the slums of London's East End or in the working-class neighborhoods of Oakland, California, where he was raised.

SOURCES FOR FURTHER STUDY

Claflin, Edward Beecher. *Jack London: Wilderness Writer*. New York: Kipling Press, 1987.

Foner, Philip S., ed. *The Social Writings of Jack London*. Secaucus, N.J.: Citadel Press, 1964.

Kershaw, Alex. *Jack London: A Life*. New York: St. Martin's Press, 1997.

Lewis, Sinclair. *Jack: A Biography of Jack London*. New York: Harper and Row, 1977.

Reader's Guide to Major Works

THE CALL OF THE WILD

Genre: Novel
Subgenre: Realistic adventure
Published: New York, 1903
Time period: 1890s
Setting: Yukon Territory, Canada

Themes and Issues. London originally wrote *The Call of the Wild* as a companion work to his short story "Batard," which portrays a vicious and vindictive sled dog. *The Call of the Wild* describes the powerful role that the environment plays in bringing out a character's essential nature. The dog Buck's return to the wilderness of his distant ancestors takes on mythic proportions as he passes into legend among the native tribes of the Yukon.

Starring Clark Gable and Loretta Young, the 1935 film version of *The Call of the Wild* was hugely successful. The author's ability to portray life as he experienced it made the reader/film viewer feel he or she was reliving the adventure, particularly those events set in Alaska and the Klondike during the gold rush era.

The Plot. Buck, half St. Bernard and half Scotch shepherd, is kidnapped from his comfortable home in the Santa Clara Valley in California by a gardener's assistant, who sells him to a dog trader to pay a gambling debt. Dogs are in high demand in the Klondike region of Canada, where a gold rush has begun and the only way to penetrate unsettled regions is by dogsled.

Buck is sent north, where he soon learns that dogs that refuse to obey are beaten into submission. Also bound for Canada is Spitz, a sadistic dog that becomes Buck's mortal enemy. Once in Alaska, Buck is purchased by Perrault and François and hitched to a sled, with Spitz at the lead. To survive, Buck must observe the other dogs, learning to bury himself in the snow to keep warm. His hatred of Spitz affects the solidarity of the team, and Spitz looks for an opportunity to attack him. However, Buck kills Spitz and becomes the lead sled dog.

After an exhausting twenty-five-hundred-mile trek, Perrault and François sell Buck and the remaining dogs to a group of new arrivals to the region who are in search of easy riches. The new owners' inexperience and mishandling of the dogs ultimately leads to disaster. Fortunately for Buck, a man named John Thornton rescues him, and Buck watches as the inept treasure hunters plunge through river ice along with their dogs and drown.

As Buck sits by the fire and hears the call of the wolves, he dreams of ancient times and of a primitive man by whom he used to sit. When the wilderness calls him, he follows a timber wolf into the forest, and they run together for hours. However, he remembers Thornton, whom he has grown to love, and returns to camp. Afterward, Buck leaves camp for days at a time, looking for the wolf and hunting his own food.

One day, he returns to camp and finds that Native Americans have killed the men and dogs. He attacks, killing many Native Americans and injuring others. After having finally killed a human, he no longer fears them unless they are armed. Buck leaves the ruined camp and confronts a pack of wolves that attack him. He fights them off, killing several. Finally, one wolf approaches, and Buck recognizes his friend. The pack accepts Buck. Later, local people begin seeing young wolves bearing Buck's markings.

Analysis. Like many of London's works, *The Call of the Wild* illustrates the importance of a character's ability to adapt to its environment. Buck survives the hardships of life in the Yukon, for which his life in California had not prepared him, through careful observation and personal courage. His ultimate victory, however, lies in his ability to draw on the primordial qualities of his nature, to recognize his connection with the wilderness, and to heed the call of his instincts.

SOURCES FOR FURTHER STUDY

De Koster, Katie, ed. *Readings on "The Call of the Wild."* San Diego, Calif.: Greenhaven Press, 1999.

Owenbey, Ray Wilson, ed. *Jack London: Essays in Criticism.* Santa Barbara, Calif.: Peregrine Smith, 1978.

Walker, Franklin. *Jack London and the Klondike.* San Marino, Calif.: Huntington Library Press, 1966.

MARTIN EDEN

Genre: Novel
Subgenre: Autobiographical novel
Published: 1908
Time period: Early 1900s
Setting: San Francisco Bay Area, California

Themes and Issues. *Martin Eden* describes the transformation of London's hero from an uneducated and rough-spoken sailor to an intelligent and successful writer. The novel is largely autobiographical, chronicling London's own development as a writer and a man. The theme of disillusionment runs deeply in this novel. Martin finds that his desire to better himself and to earn the love and respect of Ruth Morse, as well as that of the society from which she comes, brings him no satisfaction. In the end, he cannot respect the values of the fashionable society to which he has aspired, and his own success becomes a fatal source of bitterness.

The Plot. After Martin Eden rescues Arthur Morse from a barroom fight, he is invited to dine at Morse's home. There, he meets Morse's sister, Ruth, with whom he immediately falls in love. Under the spell of his desire for Ruth, Martin decides to be educated and thereby become worthy of her love.

Martin undertakes an intensive regimen of study, working nineteen hours a day and suffering privations that threaten to destroy his desire to write. He begins to succeed, and his manuscripts, previously rejected, appear in magazines. His reputation as a writer grows, and editors scurry for the rights to publish the stories they had once ignored. Once he finally achieves the success he feels is necessary to win Ruth's love, he finds that, under the influence of her family, she cannot accept him, and she even tries to discourage him from his writing.

As a writer, Martin earns worldwide fame and the respect of the upper-class world to which he has so long aspired, but he comes to see his successes as meaningless. Despite an attempt to start his life over in the Marquesas Islands, away from the society he has come to despise, he cannot escape his hopelessness. Aboard a steamship en route to the Marquesas Islands, Martin sees his only avenue of escape in death and throws himself overboard.

Analysis. London maintained that *Martin Eden* was the most misunderstood of all his books. Critics claimed that his portrayal of ordinary society, the society of Ruth Morse, was not believable. London's fellow socialists felt that he had abandoned the cause and embraced individualism, a theory that maintains that all values, rights, and duties originate in the individual. In fact, London intended *Martin Eden* to be an attack on individualism.

Although modern scholars have praised *Martin Eden* as one of London's most mature works, the novel never achieved widespread success. The story describes poignantly the struggle of a poor working-class man to better himself through education as well as the making of a literary artist. Like *The Sea-Wolf* before it, however, *Martin Eden* failed to convey London's intended message. Yet it remains an important source of information on London's own motivations as a writer.

SOURCES FOR FURTHER STUDY

Foner, Philip S. "Jack London: American Rebel." In *The Socialist Writings of Jack London*. Secaucus, N.J.: Citadel Press, 1964.

Walker, Dale L., and Jeanne Campbell Reesman. *No Mentor but Myself: Jack London on Writing and Writers*. Stanford, Calif.: Stanford University Press, 1999.

Watson, Charles N., Jr. *The Novels of Jack London: A Reappraisal*. Madison: University of Wisconsin Press, 1983.

WHITE FANG

Genre: Novel
Subgenre: Realistic adventure
Published: New York, 1906
Time period: 1890s
Setting: Yukon Territory, Canada

Themes and Issues. As *The Call of the Wild* describes a dog's return to the primitive condition of his race, *White Fang* describes the opposite journey: a wolf's transition from the harsh ancestral wilderness to unfamiliar civilization. London emphasizes once again the role of environment in shaping one's perceptions, first in White Fang's descent into savagery and finally in his return to his true nature through the kindness and love of a compassionate master.

The Plot. A pack of starving wolves pursues two dogsledders through the frozen north, systematically luring the men's dogs away from camp and killing them. After the wolves have eaten all the dogs and one of the men, they are driven away by a larger group of men who arrive in time to rescue the second sledder.

The pack leader, named One-Eye, and a she-wolf flee together into the wilderness. When the she-wolf finds a cave, she remains inside and gives birth to a litter of pups, only one of which survives. One-Eye is killed by a lynx, and the she-wolf leaves the cave to search for food. Meanwhile, the young pup begins to explore the world outside.

The pup learns about his own nature and the outside world as he experiences a series of different environments: an American Indian camp, where he is given the name White Fang and separated from his mother; a team of sled dogs, where he is hated and attacked by

Nature is everything in the fierce world of Jack London's survival tales. His characters, both animal and human, succeed only if they accept this fact and learn to adapt to their environments. Frequently, they must deal with cold and barren wildernesses like that depicted in Rockwell Kent's painting *Dogs Resting, Greenland,* ca. 1935–1937.

Charles Darwin's evolutionary theory of the survival of the fittest figures prominently in *White Fang* (1906). In this novel, London focuses on a wolf that must abandon and then reclaim its true nature in its desperate struggle to survive.

the other dogs; and Fort Yukon, where he suffers the worst abuse at the hands of Beauty Smith, who uses him as a fighting dog. White Fang becomes vicious in order to protect himself from others. When he finally faces death in his battle with a bulldog, he experiences the kindness of Weedon Scott, who takes him away from Beauty Smith.

White Fang overcomes his distrust of humans under the kind treatment of Scott. When Scott decides to return home to California, White Fang follows him to the ship. After reaching California, White Fang must adapt again to a new environment. He soon learns that his wilderness instincts do not apply in his new home. Under the guidance of Scott, he learns to get along with the family's other dogs and to refrain from killing chickens. When an escaped convict breaks into Scott's home, White Fang risks his life to save the family. He kills the man but not before receiving several gunshot wounds. As the novel closes, White Fang recovers from his injuries and fathers a litter of puppies with a sheep dog.

Analysis. Although *White Fang* never achieved the success of *The Call of the Wild*, it remains an enduring classic in its depiction of a wolf's struggle for survival against the brutality of humans and nature. The development of his identity as a creature of the wilderness is cut short by semidomestication among the Indians of the Yukon and virtually destroyed in the fighting pits at Fort Yukon. Inspired by the hatred of his fellow dogs and the inhumanity of his owners, White Fang becomes the most hateful and vicious among them.

White Fang ultimately survives, however, under the nurturing care of Scott. Moreover, just as the cruelty of his former life shaped him into a monster, the kindness of Scott and his family restores his balance. He becomes an obedient animal, but he does so willingly and with dignity.

SOURCES FOR FURTHER STUDY

Lundquist, James. *Jack London: Adventures, Ideas, and Fiction.* New York: Frederick Ungar, 1987.

Nuernberg, Susan M., ed. *The Critical Response to Jack London.* Westwood, Conn.: Greenwood Press, 1995.

Owenbey, Ray Wilson, ed. *Jack London: Essays in Criticism.* Santa Barbara, Calif.: Peregrine Smith, 1978.

Other Works

THE IRON HEEL (1907). This novel draws on Jack London's lifelong study of socialism to describe an attempted socialist revolution in a near-future America. The novel chronicles the revolutionary activities of Ernest Everhart, a charismatic socialist who believes that capitalism can be defeated at the ballot box. His crusade against the well-financed corporations that earn their profits from the misery of the underpaid working classes finds a ready following in Avis Cunningham and her father, the distinguished Berkeley professor John Cunningham. They begin to question their luxurious lifestyle and learn firsthand about factory life.

Everhart's influence spreads, and he is invited to speak before the Philomaths, an organization of the community's wealthiest businessmen. He berates their greed and warns them that the socialist revolution is imminent. In response, one of the businessmen warns Everhart that the capitalist ruling class, the

Seen here (bottom, right) with Kelley's Army, a group of unemployed workers marching in protest of economic conditions, London sympathized with the underprivileged. He recognized that their real-life battle against poverty and injustice was as compelling and dangerous as any in his fiction.

"iron heel," will crush any attempt to seize its control. The threat of violence is soon realized as Dr. Cunningham loses his position at the university, a priest who has embraced socialism is committed to an asylum, and socialist leaders are arrested or simply disappear.

The workers begin to fight back by organizing a revolt against the growing oppression of the capitalist oligarchy. As workers take to the streets of Chicago, they do not realize that a professional army has been sent to quell the uprising. The workers are massacred in the streets, and the city is devastated. Afterward, the workers begin an underground movement, organized by Everhart and other socialist leaders who are now in prison. The manuscript ends abruptly with Avis in hiding and the country on the threshold of a second revolution.

When it was published in 1908, critics dismissed *The Iron Heel* as mere sensationalism. Many socialists as well found the work troubling, particularly London's efforts to show that a peaceful transition from capitalism to socialism was impossible. The novel also suffers artistically in its early depiction of Ernest Everhart as little more than an idealized figurehead. However, the oligarchy's systematic suppression of democracy and its attempt to destroy all who oppose its power suggest comparisons to the rise of fascist regimes in the decades following London's death.

THE SEA-WOLF (1904). London claimed that this novel was his attempt to refute Friedrich Nietzsche's philosophical ideal of the "superman." Henry Van Weyden, an upper-class gentleman and writer, is pitched overboard when the ferry he is riding collides with another ship on San Francisco Bay. He is rescued by the crew of a sealing vessel called the *Ghost*, on its way to Japan. Its captain, Wolf Larsen, refuses to turn back to San Francisco and forces Van Weyden to join the crew.

With no previous sailing experience and unaccustomed to physical labor, Van Weyden must learn to cope with the hardships of sea life. He soon discovers, however, that his greatest threat is Larsen, who rules the ship through cruelty, believing he can overcome any difficulty by the strength of his body and the superiority of his mind.

Off Japan, Larsen rescues survivors of another shipwreck, who include a young woman named Maud Brewster. Van Weyden, fearing for the woman's safety and troubled by the growing insanity aboard the *Ghost*, flees with her aboard a small boat, and they wash ashore on an uninhabited island. After several days, Van Weyden finds the *Ghost* beached on the island shore with its masts shattered. Like the damaged ship, Larsen himself has lost much of his vigor. Completely alone, he is now blind and partially paralyzed by a stroke.

Van Weyden and Brewster repair the *Ghost* for their departure from the island while Larsen loses all control of his body, unable even to speak. The man who once took pride in his superior strength and cruelty is reduced to com-

Rockwell Kent's 1921 painting *The Trapper* (Whitney Museum of American Art) echoes the hostile environment of the Yukon found in "To Build a Fire," a truly classic American short story and one of London's best.

plete impotence. While sailing back to civilization, the once indomitable Captain Larsen dies.

Critics failed to see London's critique of Nietzsche in *The Sea-Wolf*, but the novel became an instant best-seller. Its strength resides in the contrast between Larsen and Van Weyden. Van Weyden adapts to his new environment aboard the *Ghost*, learning the skills that will ensure his survival, but Larsen becomes a victim of his own isolation. He is unable to maintain control of the *Ghost* and its crew, and in the end he loses control of himself.

"TO BUILD A FIRE" (1900). In this short story, an unnamed gold hunter travels on foot through the frozen landscape of the Yukon. New to the region, he travels alone in the cold, against the advice of an experienced Yukon man. A native Husky dog follows at his heels as the man frequently rubs his frozen cheeks and slaps his hands together to fight the cold.

The man watches carefully for thin patches of ice that cover underground springs along the trail. He knows that if he breaks through the ice and gets wet, he must stop and build a fire to dry himself or risk freezing to death. Eventually, the man does break through the ice. He tries to build a fire and succeeds briefly, until the snow clinging to a tree branch above falls and extinguishes the flames. He tries again, this time well away from the trees, but his fingers are frozen, and he fails. In desperation, he begins to run, but he cannot feel his feet and collapses from exhaustion. The dog senses the man's fate and continues along the trail.

Early in the story, London states that the unnamed traveler lacks imagination. He does not understand the nature of the cold or the frailty of human beings against it. London's theme—that of the man's struggle against a hostile environment—is clearly drawn throughout the story. The cold itself takes on the qualities of a main character in the story as it pursues the naïve traveler, striking him when he removes his mittens, waiting for him to make the slightest mistake. The story's compact narrative and the unity of its various elements have made "To Build a Fire" a widely read classic of the American short-story genre and one of London's greatest works of short fiction.

Resources

Major collections of Jack London's manuscripts reside in numerous institutions, including the Huntington Library in San Marino, California, and the Bancroft Library at the University of California at Berkeley. Other important sources of information on the life and work of Jack London include the following:

Jack London Collection. Maintained by the University of California at Berkeley, this collection includes a comprehensive online digital library with electronic texts of London's works, photographs of London and his family and friends, personal and official documents (including London's death certificate), resources for students and teachers, and much more. (http://www.sunsite.lib.berkeley.edu/London)

Jack London Society. An international nonprofit organization created in 1990, the Jack London Society publishes a biannual newsletter, *The Call*, with arti-cles about London's life and work, notices of recent publications, and news about member activities. The society holds a symposium every two years that includes the presentation of formal papers, workshops, and social events. (http://www.sunsite.berkeley.edu/London/Organizations/jl_society.html)

Jack London State Historical Park. Created in 1959 when the State of California acquired forty acres of London's fourteen-hundred-acre Beauty Ranch, the park today covers eight hundred acres and contains the gravesites of London and his second wife, the ruins of Wolf House, Charmian's House of Happy Walls (built after London's death and now a museum), and portions of Beauty Ranch, including the cottage where London wrote most of his later work. (http://www.parks.sonoma.net/JLPark.htm)

PHILIP BADER

Archibald MacLeish

BORN: May 7, 1892, Glencoe, Illinois
DIED: April 20, 1982, Boston, Massachusetts
IDENTIFICATION: Twentieth-century American poet, playwright, essayist, teacher, and public servant.

Archibald MacLeish emerged as a major American poet in the 1920s and 1930s and went on to publish more than forty books in his long literary life. His unique contribution to poetry was recognized after he won a Pulitzer Prize in Poetry for *Conquistador* (1932) and published *Poems, 1924–1933* (1933). He is perhaps most significant for combining a literary career with a lifetime in public service. He played important roles in government, serving as an administrator, spokesman, and diplomat, as well as in education, teaching at Harvard University for almost fifteen years.

The Writer's Life

Archibald MacLeish was born on May 7, 1892, in Glencoe, Illinois. His father, Andrew MacLeish, was a well-to-do retailer. His mother, Martha Hillard MacLeish, had been a professor and president of Rockford College. An easterner from Connecticut, she sent MacLeish back east, in 1907, to the Hotchkiss School. MacLeish wrote poetry at Hotchkiss and later at Yale University, where he also played football, captained the water polo team, and joined the prestigious Skull and Bones Society. He was elected class poet and a member of Phi Beta Kappa. In 1915 he was named the outstanding graduating senior. MacLeish did not find the schools he attended to be intellectually stimulating, but they provided him with friends and connections that served him well later in life.

At Yale, MacLeish decided that he would marry Ada Hitchcock, whom he had met at Hotchkiss, and that he would earn a living as a lawyer while writing poetry in his spare time. He entered Harvard Law School in 1915. On June 21, 1916, he married Ada, hoping that two could live as cheaply as one on the allowance his father provided while MacLeish was in law school. He found law school, unlike Yale, to be an exciting intellectual challenge.

After the United States entered World War I in 1917, MacLeish joined Yale's army ambulance unit as a private and then transferred to the field artillery and was commissioned. By the end of the war, he was a captain. Less than a month before the Armistice, Archibald's much-loved younger brother, Kenneth, a fighter pilot, was lost.

MacLeish received his law degree in 1919. Rejecting offers from several law offices, he supported himself and Ada by teaching at Harvard University and Northeastern University, as well as writing for *Time* magazine. Meanwhile, he was writing a good deal of poetry. In 1921, however, he did join a Boston law firm in order to earn more money. He was a very capable lawyer and enjoyed legal work. However, he found that law left him too little time for poetry, so in 1923 he went to the firm's senior partner to resign. By an extraordinary coincidence, MacLeish found the partners assembled and

MacLeish around 1915 as a student at Yale University in New Haven, Connecticut, where he distinguished himself both in scholastics and athletics.

The poet and his wife moved to Paris in 1923. Among the many artists and writers he met there was Pablo Picasso, the renowned Spanish painter of this 1901 painting, *Wandering Acrobats* (Pushkin Museum of Fine Arts, Moscow).

waiting to offer him a partnership. His resignation was extremely awkward.

Paris. After his resignation, MacLeish moved his family to Paris, France, in order to reach the heart of the postwar artistic renaissance. Here he encountered artists such as the Spanish painter and sculptor Pablo Picasso, the Russian composer Igor Stravinsky, the Irish writer James Joyce, and the American expatriates. MacLeish objected to the term *expatriates*, because he and the others continued to regard themselves as Americans. MacLeish knew many artists and writers in Paris socially, although he did not discuss their art with them.

MacLeish enjoyed a particularly close friendship with the American writer Ernest Hemingway. While Ada pursued an active career as a concert soprano, MacLeish learned the craft of poetry. He read Dante in the original, read widely the new poetry of the 1920s, and wrote a great deal. He made little money from his writing, but his father renewed his allowance to the family, and Ada also brought in a sizable income with her singing. In *Streets in the Moon* (1926), MacLeish was finally writing the kind of poetry he wanted to write. Although they were happy in France, the MacLeishes decided to return to the United States in 1928.

Return to the United States. The MacLeishes bought Uphill Farm in the Berkshire foothills of Conway, Massachusetts. The house was in such bad shape and the first winter so harsh that MacLeish took his family to his mother's home in Illinois. He then went on to retrace the route of the Spanish conquistador Hernán Cortés during the conquest of Mexico so that he could work more effectively on his American epic *Conquistador*. In 1929

Writing about politics and business for *Fortune Magazine* paid his bills, but writing about U.S. issues also instilled the patriotism that would permeate his work. The above photograph of MacLeish was taken in October of 1939, shortly after he accepted his position as librarian of Congress. He was at first reluctant to discuss his plans for his new role, saying "I've barely got my chair warmed here. It would be impertinent for me to try to talk about what I'm going to change in a great institution like this."

MacLeish agreed to write for *Fortune* magazine, with the understanding that he would work on a yearly basis only until he had earned enough to pay his bills. Working for *Fortune* taught him a great deal about business, politics, and living conditions in the United States and abroad.

During the 1930s MacLeish found himself engaged in political controversy. Sympathetic with the causes of the Left, he nonetheless felt that a poet should remain apart from partisan politics. His refusal to propagandize became itself a political position. By the end of the 1930s, his views were more clearly and more vocally anticommunist and antifascist. His experience writing on U.S. issues for *Fortune* magazine inspired the growing patriotism reflected in all of his writing.

In 1939 MacLeish was unexpectedly asked by President Franklin D. Roosevelt to become librarian of Congress. Although he foresaw that the position would take him from his writing, he reluctantly accepted and spearheaded a sweeping reorganization of the Library of

HIGHLIGHTS IN MACLEISH'S LIFE

1892   Archibald MacLeish is born on May 7 in Glencoe, Illinois.

1911   Graduates from the Hotchkiss School and enters Yale University.

1915   Graduates from Yale and enters Harvard Law School.

1916   Marries Ada Hitchcock.

1917   Joins the U.S. Army and serves in France; publishes book of poetry, *Tower of Ivory*.

1919   Leaves army as a captain; earns law degree from Harvard, where he begins teaching.

1921   Begins practicing law at a Boston firm.

1923   Leaves law firm and moves with family to Paris, France, to concentrate on poetry.

1928   Returns to United States; buys Uphill Farm in Conway, Massachusetts.

1929   Accepts a position with *Fortune* magazine.

1932   Publishes epic poem *Conquistador*.

1933   Awarded a Pulitzer Prize for *Conquistador*; publishes *Poems, 1924–1933*.

1939   Appointed Librarian of Congress.

1941   Appointed director of the U.S. Office of Facts and Figures; continues as Librarian of Congress.

1944   Leaves the Library of Congress; appointed assistant secretary of state.

1945   Leaves the U.S. State Department; active in founding the United Nations.

1949   Joins the Harvard faculty as Boylston Professor of Rhetoric and Oratory, teaching until 1962.

1952   Publishes *Collected Poems, 1917–1952*.

1953   Awarded a second Pulitzer Prize for poetry, the Bollingen Prize for poetry, the Shelley Memorial Award, and the National Book Award in poetry; elected president of the American Academy of Arts and Sciences.

1958   Publishes *J.B.: A Play in Verse*, which wins a Tony Award in drama and a Pulitzer Prize for drama.

1961   Publishes *Poetry and Experience*.

1976   Publishes *New and Collected Poems, 1917–1976*.

1982   Dies on April 20.

1985   *Collected Poems, 1917–1982* is published posthumously.

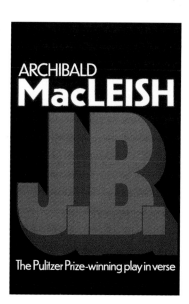

ARCHIBALD **MacLEISH**

J.B.

The Pulitzer Prize-winning play in verse

Congress. He also used his position to speak forcefully against censorship. Subsequently he helped to establish and administer government information offices, worked as a speechwriter for Roosevelt, and helped in the administration's planning for peace—all while continuing as Librarian of Congress. In 1944 he resigned from that position, only to be appointed assistant secretary of state for public and cultural relations. In the immediate postwar period, MacLeish was involved in the creation of the United Nations and the establishment of the United Nations Educational, Scientific, and Cultural Organization (UNESCO).

Return to Harvard. Although MacLeish left Washington regretting his long silence as a poet, he had to readjust before finding his voice once again in *Actfive and Other Poems* (1948). In 1949 he was named Boylston Professor of Rhetoric and Oratory at Harvard. There he taught writing and poetry, later publishing the distilled insights of his poetry course in *Poetry and Experience* (1961). At Harvard, he introduced his students to many of his prominent acquaintances.

MacLeish wrote prolifically while at Harvard, publishing his prizewinning *Collected Poems, 1917–1952* (1952) and *J.B.: A Play in Verse* (1958), among other major works. He also remained active in public affairs, vigorously opposing Senator Joseph McCarthy's crusade of the early 1950s against alleged communists in government and the arts. MacLeish finally retired—because university policy required him to—when he reached seventy. He later regarded his thirteen years at Harvard as the happiest period of his life.

The MacLeishes returned to Conway but, as always, continued to travel widely. Throughout the 1960s and 1970s, MacLeish wrote both poetry and drama and gave public readings of his work. In his eighties, he was still vigorous and looking forward to further work. His health began to fail around 1980, and he died at Massachusetts General Hospital, in Boston, on April 20, 1982. A symposium that had been planned as a ninetieth-birthday celebration for MacLeish was held instead as a memorial. There, a tribute from the poet Richard Wilbur was read: "Not all good poets are good men, but Archie was always both."

MacLeish wore many hats in his lifetime. First and foremost a poet, he was also a speechwriter for President Franklin Delano Roosevelt and Boylston Professor of Rhetoric and Oratory at Harvard from 1949 to 1962.

The Writer's Work

Much of the poetry that Archibald MacLeish wrote at Hotchkiss imitated the work of the late-nineteenth-century British poet Algernon Charles Swinburne. MacLeish's college poetry was traditional in form and conventional in sentiment. Many of the poems that he wrote in Paris were also derivative, but his models were the modernists T. S. Eliot and Ezra Pound instead of the Victorians. Many of his Paris poems, like those of his contemporaries, express disillusionment—with materialism and superficiality, with political dogmas, and with traditional religion and philosophy. As MacLeish found his own voice, he regarded nothing less than the whole of human experience as his topic.

Themes. Over the course of his career MacLeish wrote many poems dealing with universal subjects: the appreciation of nature; the experiences of love, friendship, death, and grief; the nature of time; and humankind's relationship to God. Many of his short lyrics are evocations of nature, leaning more toward the romanticism of the poet William Wordsworth than the realism of Robert Frost.

Not conventionally religious, MacLeish was deeply interested in religious questions. He treated the theme of mortality in varied ways, sometimes focusing only on the physical facts of death, sometimes on enduring memories, sometimes on a faith in darkly apprehended immortality. MacLeish commonly presents God as inscrutable, arbitrary, and oppressive.

MacLeish's love poetry explores commitment, infidelity, jealousy, disillusionment, reconciliation, and the peace of mature companionship. Time tends to be seen as ominous: the inexorable destroyer of love, beauty, and all that is precious in life. Paradoxically, time is also a force to be transcended through memory and art.

In the 1930s MacLeish began to deal with political topics in his work, including the suffering of victims and the dignity of labor, the superficiality and hypocrisy of demagogues, the threats posed by extremists of the Left and the Right, the duties of citizenship, and the value of Jeffersonian ideals.

Joellyn Duesberry's 1985 oil painting *Trees in March, Millbrook* evokes the early-nineteenth-century romantic awareness and appreciation of nature that colored much of the poet's work.

SOME INSPIRATIONS BEHIND MACLEISH'S WORK

For a time at least, Archibald MacLeish thought that his poems began with "a sort of pattern of rhythm . . . which had no relation to words at all." Conscious of the rhythmic pattern, he would try to find the words to fill it and keep it going. MacLeish's sense of rhythm may have been fostered by his mother, who read aloud to him and his siblings during their childhood, beginning with a selection such as Charles Kingsley's *The Water Babies* (1863) and continuing with stories and psalms from the King James version of the Bible, William Shakespeare, and John Aitken Carlyle's translation of Dante.

While MacLeish's theory of rhythmic inspiration for writing may have worked for him, it apparently did not work as well for a colleague on a League of Nations commission to Persia who asked for help in writing a section of the commission's report. MacLeish, no expert on the topic, agreed to write a model. "Of course it will be all wrong," he said. "It will be nonsense; but you just follow my sentences and put in the right words." MacLeish was surprised, when the report came out, to see not only the rhythms but also all of the nonsense words of his sentences. Images from this trip to Persia, incidentally, combined with MacLeish's strong emotional response to an illness of his father to produce "You, Andrew Marvell," one of the very few poems MacLeish ever wrote in a single day.

Another of MacLeish's poems rooted in experience is the sonnet "The End of the World," which he began after taking his family to a traveling French circus. The images described in the first seven lines are all typical of the small European circuses that MacLeish knew. The last half of the poem is imagined; MacLeish's imagination here may have been helped by the torchlight in the circus tent, which he found strongly suggestive of death, and by the threatening force of Atlantic Ocean gales on the circus tents and their rigging. The poem's rhythm, "very unsonnetlike," according to MacLeish, came from the phrase "quite unexpectedly," which repeated in his head and with which he begins both the poem's first line and its pivotal eighth line.

MacLeish responded strongly to sense impressions. "We go to our grave by way of door knobs and banisters and buttons and rough cloth and smooth cloth," he observed. Many of his poems are built on vivid sense impressions. Asked about the inspiration for "Broken Promise," a poem about love and betrayal, he responded that all poems were not autobiographical. "Broken Promise" begins not with an affair but with the image of a star seen through an open doorway inside of which MacLeish remembered standing completely alone one night in the south of France.

MacLeish sometimes drew from real-life experience. His sonnet "The End of the World" was inspired by a family trip to a traveling French circus.

Forms and Techniques. Beginning with his work in Paris, MacLeish explored a variety of poetic forms and techniques, including traditional stanzaic forms, blank verse, and free verse. Even before he went to Paris, he had been interested in dramatic poetry. In the 1930s he learned to write for the stage and became a pioneer in radio drama, in which he remained interested to the very end of his career. An extraordinarily versatile writer, he also experimented with ballet; opera; *son et lumière*, outdoor narrative presentations with light and sound effects; and film and television scripts.

BIBLIOGRAPHY

Atkinson, Brooks, et al. *Pembroke Magazine* 7 (1976): 3–146.

Barber, David. "In Search of an `Image of Mankind': The Public Poetry and Prose of Archibald MacLeish." *American Studies* 29 (Fall 1988): 31–56.

Commager, Henry Steele, et al. *Massachusetts Review* 23 (Winter 1982).

Donaldson, Scott. *Archibald MacLeish: An American Life.* Boston: Houghton Mifflin, 1992.

Drabeck, Bernard A., and Helen E. Ellis, eds. *Archibald MacLeish: Reflections.* Amherst: University of Massachusetts Press, 1986.

Drabeck, Bernard A., Helen E. Ellis, and Seymour Rudin, eds. *Proceedings of the Archibald MacLeish Symposium, May 7–8, 1982.* Lanham, Md.: University Press of America, 1988.

Drabeck, Bernard A., and Helen E. Ellis with Margaret E. C. Howland. *Archibald MacLeish: A Selectively Annotated Bibliography.* Lanham, Md.: Scarecrow Press, 1995.

Falk, Signi Lenea. *Archibald MacLeish.* New York: Twayne Publishers, 1965.

Mullaly, Edward J. *Archibald MacLeish: A Checklist.* Kent, Ohio: Kent State University Press, 1973.

Newcomb, John Timberman. "Archibald MacLeish and the Poetics of Public Speech: A Critique of High Modernism." *Journal of the MidWest Modern Language Association* 23 (Spring 1990): 9–28.

Smith, Grover. *Archibald MacLeish.* Minneapolis: University of Minnesota Press, 1971.

The whole of human experience was MacLeish's subject matter, but politics emerged as a topic in his work in the 1930s. Clifford Goodenough's 1986 painting *Still Life* reflects the poet's warnings against extremists of both the Left and Right.

Reader's Guide to Major Works

COLLECTED POEMS, 1917–1982

Genre: Poetry
Subgenre: Lyric and epic poetry
Published: Boston, 1985
Time period: Various historical eras
Setting: Europe; Mexico; United States

Themes and Issues. *Collected Poems* contains a selection of poems representing MacLeish's long career, including "Conquistador," the long poem that won MacLeish his first Pulitzer Prize, as well as many lyrics, among which are MacLeish's best known and most thought-provoking poems.

The Poems. While reading Bernal Díaz del Castillo's eyewitness narrative of the attempted conquest of the Mexican Aztecs by the Spanish, MacLeish was struck by its value as a metaphor for the conquest of the New World. He had started work on *Conquistador*, a poem that is epic in subject, characters, length, and style. The poem's narrator is Díaz in old age, remembering the exploits of his youth, when he followed the Spanish conquistador Hernán Cortés. The use of Díaz, a common soldier, as the narrator reflects MacLeish's democratic values. Particularly at the beginning, MacLeish's phrases and sentences are fragmentary, like those actually found in Díaz's decayed manuscript.

MacLeish's narrative advances as an old man recalls his memories in a series of discontinuous but vivid, emotionally intense vignettes. The conquest of Mexico is presented as a kind of rape in which both Spaniards and Indians lose the unperceived, almost-grasped opportunity for an innocent, idyllic coexistence and find instead betrayal, destruction, disillusionment, and death.

MacLeish's shorter poems are his most widely read works. One such poem in this collection is the sonnet "The End of the World," which begins with the rather cruel

but whimsical image of the armless ambidexterian and ends with the image of the absolutely empty night sky. The meter of the poem imitates a showman's timing. The dactylic rhythm moves the first half of the poem along quickly, and the slower rhythm of the last lines is emphatic, as is the poem's periodic sentence structure. Cosmic emptiness is emphasized, but against this theme of negation is the assertion of

In 1698, the artist Gonzalez trumpeted the conquest of Mexico in *Cortés Enters Mexico* (Mus. de America, Madrid). *Conquistador*, MacLeish's 1932 epic poem for which he won his first Pulitzer Prize in 1933, sees events very differently.

the poem's form—a sonnet—which epitomizes human rationality and control.

"Memorial Rain" is one of many poems that MacLeish wrote about his brother Kenneth's death in World War I. The poem describes MacLeish's visit to Kenneth's grave in Belgium on Memorial Day in 1924, when the American ambassador made a speech. The ambassador's words are windy—pompous, trite, and insincere—but blowing through the cemetery is a very real wind. Unlike the speech, this wind has meaning. The wind brings rain, which puts an end to the Memorial Day observances. It is a life-giving rain, restoring the dry grass of the cemetery and reaching down through the earth to Kenneth's waiting bones. MacLeish had come to believe that Kenneth had died for nothing in a politician's war, and "Memorial Rain" is a very bitter poem. More affirmative is the much later "For the Anniversary of My Mother's Death," which concludes with the assurance that even in the earth of the grave, the "Sea-beat" of life goes on, washing "the last, far-off, profound / Dark shore and deepest caves."

MacLeish's poem "You, Andrew Marvell" alludes to Marvell's poem "To His Coy Mistress,"

POETRY

1915 Songs for a Summer's Day
1917 Tower of Ivory
1924 The Happy Marriage
1925 The Pot of Earth
1926 Streets in the Moon
1928 The Hamlet of A. MacLeish
1929 Einstein
1930 New Found Land: Fourteen Poems
1932 Conquistador
1933 Poems, 1924–1933
1933 Frescoes for Mr. Rockefeller's City
1936 Public Speech
1938 Land of the Free
1939 America Was Promises
1948 Brave New World
1948 Actfive and Other Poems
1952 Collected Poems, 1917–1952
1952 New Poems, 1951–1952
1954 Songs for Eve
1962 The Collected Poems of Archibald MacLeish
1968 The Wild Old Wicked Man and Other Poems

1972 The Human Season: Selected Poems, 1926–1972
1976 New and Collected Poems, 1917–1976
1978 On the Beaches of the Moon
1985 Collected Poems, 1917–1982

PLAYS

1925 The Pot of Earth
1926 Nobodaddy: A Play
1935 Panic: A Play in Verse
1937 The Fall of the City: A Verse Play for Radio
1938 Air Raid: A Verse Play for Radio
1952 The Trojan Horse: A Play
1953 This Music Crept by Me Upon the Waters
1958 J.B.: A Play in Verse
1965 Herakles: A Play in Verse
1971 Scratch
1980 Six Plays

NONFICTION

1932 Housing America
1936 Jews in America
1937 Background of War
1940 The Irresponsibles: A Declaration

1941 The American Cause
1941 A Time to Speak: The Selected Prose of Archibald MacLeish
1942 American Opinion and the War
1943 A Time to Act: Selected Addresses
1950 Poetry and Opinion: The "Pisan Cantos" of Ezra Pound
1951 Freedom Is the Right to Choose: An Inquiry into the Battle for the American Future
1961 Poetry and Experience
1964 The Dialogues of Archibald MacLeish and Mark Van Doren
1965 The Eleanor Roosevelt Story
1968 A Continuing Journey
1968 The Great American Frustration
1971 Champion of a Cause: Essays and Addresses on Librarianship
1978 Riders on the Earth: Essays and Reminiscences
1983 Letters of Archibald MacLeish: 1970–1982, ed. R. H. Winnick

which opens "Had we but world enough, and time, / This coyness, lady, were no crime." and begins its second section "But at my back I always hear / Time's winged chariot hurrying near." MacLeish's poem describes the inexorable progress of darkness, with its connotations of death and extinction, across the face of the earth, reaching from the Eastern cradles of civilization toward the New World and the speaker—and the reader. The poem is one long sentence, incomplete but with an inescapable conclusion.

"American Letter," written soon after MacLeish's return to the United States, expresses his nostalgia for France, "The red roofs and the olives, / And the foreign words . . ." paradoxically make France feel like home. However, he is affirming his American identity when he asserts, "This . . . is our land. . . / Here we must eat our salt or our bones starve." Back in Europe, F. Scott Fitzgerald found this poem so meaningful that he memorized much of it. MacLeish followed "American Letter" with other poems about his feelings for the United States, including "Landscape as a Nude," which pictures the United States as a woman—a beautiful, strong, fruitful individual—a bold but effective metaphor.

Among MacLeish's many poems about love is "What Any Lover Learns," a poem that also serves as an evocation of the New England landscape. The poem is built on a single, simple metaphor comparing the relationship between lovers to one of New England's swift little rivers running over the bedrock. The river is heavy, insinuating itself into every crevice, pressing down—but the stone does not yield. "River does not run," the poem says, "What runs, / Swirling and leaping into sun, is stone's / Refusal of the river, not the river."

MacLeish's most famous poem, "Ars Poetica," is a series of beautiful and evocative images. Its last two lines surely are among the most often-quoted lines in the English language: "A poem should not mean / But be." These lines have

Man on Top of the World, a 1995 oil painting by Adam Straus, captures the whimsical, yet unsettling tone of MacLeish's 1961 work of nonfiction, *Poetry and Experience*.

been read as a statement of MacLeish's aesthetic; such an interpretation, however, gives the poem a meaning, causing it to violate its own ideal. If the poem is regarded as merely a description of itself alone, the contradiction disappears. MacLeish's poetry, while firmly grounded in strong images, is not meaningless.

At the end of *Poetry and Experience*, MacLeish declares, "To face the truth of the passing away of the world and make a song of it, to make beauty of it, is not to solve the riddle of our mortal lives but perhaps to accomplish something more." The best of MacLeish's *Collected Poems* are such accomplishments.

SOURCES FOR FURTHER STUDY

Carruth, Hayden. "Homage to A. MacLeish." *Virginia Quarterly Review* 53 (Winter 1977): 146–154.

Pritchard, William H. "MacLeish Revisited." *Poetry* 141 (February 1983): 291–301.

Wilbur, Richard. "Collected Poems." *New England Quarterly* 26 (March 1953): 117–121.

J.B.: A PLAY IN VERSE

Genre: Verse drama
Subgenre: Morality play
Published: Boston, 1958
Time period: Mid–twentieth century
Setting: New England

Themes and Issues. Archibald MacLeish personally experienced World War II's random destruction in London, and he heard of the equally arbitrary devastation in Dresden and Hiroshima, where thousands of innocent civilians suffered. His brooding on this random, and therefore meaningless, human suffering led him to the biblical Old Testament Book of Job and ultimately to the writing of his play *J.B.*, a twentieth-century retelling of Job's story.

The Plot. In a circus tent, Mr. Zuss and Nickles, two disillusioned, out-of-work actors, assume the roles of God and Satan in the story of Job and find appropriate masks through which to act. Nickles, appalled at meaningless suffering, plays Satan. Zuss, indifferent to suffering and justice, plays God. Someone else will play Job, he assures Nickles—there are so many Jobs. J.B. (Job) appears with his family in the arena, and his story unfolds before Nickles and Zuss, a play within the play.

J.B., a wealthy New England banker and a faultless man, his wife, Sarah, and their five children all live comfortably and contentedly. Sarah believes that the family members have earned their good fortune by good works and is afraid that they may somehow cease to deserve it. J.B. attributes their luck not to deserving but to God's favor, on which he relies.

Zuss and Nickles will test J.B.'s piety, but, a Distant Voice admonishes them, J.B. himself must not be harmed. J.B.'s children, all innocent, die senselessly: one in a wartime blunder after the fighting is over, two in an automobile accident caused by a drunk driver, the youngest girl at the hands of a dope-crazed child molester, and the last daughter in an explosion that destroys J.B.'s bank. J.B. responds,

MacLeish's 1958 *J.B.: A Play in Verse* is a retelling of the Old Testament story. Though very different from Jusepe de Ribera's *Job* (Galleria Nazionale, Parma, Italy), MacLeish's New England banker bears his twentieth-century sorrows equally piously.

"The Lord giveth . . . the Lord taketh away," but when he demands that Sarah repeat these words, she shrieks that the Lord kills. J.B. is resolute, saying, "Blessed be the name of the Lord."

The test becomes more rigorous; now J.B., who is covered with sores, and Sarah are among the few survivors of catastrophe. Sarah calls God their enemy; J.B. instead tries to understand wherein his own guilt lies. Sarah demands that J.B. curse God and die. When J.B. insists instead that guilt is necessary, that it is what makes God thinkable, Sarah leaves him.

At this point the play's set changes—the circus tent is no longer visible. J.B., alone and blind, is visited by three Comforters. The first, Bildad, is a marxist for whom individual guilt and innocence are irrelevant and only social history counts. Eliphaz is a psychiatrist who calls guilt an illusion and a sickness. Zophar, a priest, insists that guilt is no illusion; all people are guilty because they are human.

J.B. rejects the counsel of all three Comforters, finding the notion that all of humankind is inherently guilty—created that way

J.B. and his wife, Sarah, with Nickles (Satan) and Zuss (God) in the background in a scene from *J.B.*, the poet's contemporary morality play.

by God—the cruelest comfort of all. He cries out to God. After a long silence the Distant Voice challenges the presumption of ignorant men who would presume to instruct the Almighty, and the Comforters uncomfortably depart. J.B. understands finally that his guilt is that he is not God; he abhors himself and repents.

Nickles is disgusted with Job's acquiescence; Zuss, who has played God, seems deflated even in his triumph, but the story goes on, as it must. J.B. is restored. His sores are healed. Sarah returns. J.B. reproaches her for leaving, and she answers that when he wanted justice, all she could offer was love. "Blow on the coal of the heart," she urges J.B., "and we'll see by and by. "

Analysis. In the *New York Times* a few days before *J.B.* opened on Broadway, MacLeish wrote that he was trying to come to terms with the horrors of war, which indiscriminately destroys cities and people, with no discernable cause. That MacLeish perceived these disasters with personal poignancy is suggested by the similarity between the fate of J.B.'s first son, death in a military accident after an armistice, and that of MacLeish's brother Kenneth, a pilot lost shortly before the end of the war, whose body was found two months later, with no visible wound, not far from his intact plane. Kenneth's death remained a painful mystery.

The circus-tent setting of the play's beginning is reminiscent of MacLeish's poem "The End of the World." However, above the poem's tent is nothingness. God presides over the tent in *J.B.*—not only in the form of Zuss behind the God-mask but also in the presence behind the Distant Voice. Speaking for God, Zuss may be knowing, but he is not omnipotent, and he is clearly indifferent to human suffering. The Distant Voice teaches J.B. both his own limitations and the Creator's knowledge and power. Nonetheless, human love, not God, prevails. In the play, J.B. recognizes that life's only certainty is "love's inevitable heartbreak." He is, however, determined to go on—ignorant, fearful, but persistent—"and still live . . . still love."

Some theatergoers criticized *J.B.* for lacking fully developed characters. However, just as the biblical Job is a universal figure, and not an individual like Moses or David, so J.B. is not a tragic hero like Hamlet but rather the Everyman protagonist of a morality play. The representational style of the stage set, the device of the play within the play, the masks that Zuss and Nickles use, the Distant Voice, the use of poetry for the dialogue—all make this not a realistic drama but one representing universal truth. The play's truth is that although love conquers nothing, it does affirm life, even in extremity.

SOURCES FOR FURTHER STUDY

Atkinson, Brooks. "Archibald MacLeish's New Play, `J.B.'" *New York Times*, April 24, 1958, p. 37.

_____. "MacLeish's `J.B.'" *New York Times*, December 12, 1958, p. 2.

Ciardi, John. "Birth of a Classic." *Saturday Review*, March 8, 1958, pp. 11–12.

Hall, Donald. "Archibald MacLeish: On Being a Poet in the Theater." *Horizon* 2 (1960): 48–56.

Kazan, Elia, et al. "The Staging of a Play." *Esquire* 51 (1959): 144–158.

MacLeish, Archibald. "About a Trespass on a Monument." *New York Times*, December 7, 1958, p. 5.

Other Works

THE FALL OF THE CITY (1937). This verse play for radio was the first of its kind in the United States. MacLeish was excited by the potential of radio, which relies almost totally on the word, to stimulate the imagination. In the printed text, the play's action is set in Tenochtitlán, during the time of Cortés. In performance, neither time nor place was specified. The action begins with the announcer's description of a frightened crowd awaiting an

Lucien Levy-Dhurmer's 1986 image *Eve*. Unlike the biblical first woman, the protagonist of MacLeish's 1954 *Songs for Eve* ascends into understanding instead of falling into shame.

The Fall of the City to be prophetic; less than a year after its first performance came the Anschluss, Germany's annexation of Austria prior to the beginning of World War II. In 1937 the play was certainly antifascist in its thrust, but its import is not limited to the politics of the 1930s.

SONGS FOR EVE (1954). *Songs for Eve*, first published in 1954 and reprinted in *Collected Poems, 1917–1982*, is a sequence of twenty-eight short lyrics, most of which are spoken by or addressed to Eve, the biblical first woman and the protagonist. The style of the sequence is symbolic and suggestive rather than explicit; the songs are statements and counter-statements. Those of the serpent are cynical and conventional. Adam's songs reflect not only a growing self-awareness but also a misunderstanding of the soul as something distinct from the body. Eve understands body and soul to be one and perceives eternity and infinity beyond the limitations of place and time that govern animal existence. She eats the apple not to fall into sin, guilt, and death but rather to ascend into understanding, freedom, and immortality. In this work, as in his very early *Nobodaddy* (1926) and his later *J.B.*, MacLeish has adapted a scriptural story for his own purpose—in this case, an optimistic affirmation of human potential.

omen. An oracular voice from a tomb prophesies that to take a master, the free men of the city will surrender their freedom and later pay in blood for their choice. Messengers now warn the crowd of the approach of the conqueror. The terrified crowd turns against its leaders only to be pacified by priests. An aged general tries to encourage resistance, but his urging is in vain. When the armor-clad figure of the conqueror finally appears, the crowd submits, even though, as the announcer reports, "The helmet is hollow! / . . . The armor is empty!"

The theme of the play reiterates that of MacLeish's earlier, unsuccessful stage play *Panic* (1935). A deterministic belief in catastrophe can disarm free will and become a self-fulfilling prophecy, but the strong person's promise is delusion; true strength requires people's unity and courage. In the late 1930s, audiences found

THIS MUSIC CREPT BY ME UPON THE WATERS (1953). For many years the MacLeishes spent their winters on the Caribbean island of Antigua in the British West

Indies. MacLeish enjoyed the company of the literate rich who flocked there—although not uncritically. His experiences on Antigua and elsewhere impressed upon him the ability of the rich in the age of air travel to pursue pleasure at any time virtually anywhere in the world.

The title of *This Music Crept by Me Upon the Waters* alludes to Shakespeare's *Tempest*. The play takes place on an island in the Antilles, which seems enchanted under a full moon. Several couples assemble for a dinner party. Although they are wealthy and privileged, several of them are superficial and discontented. In a moment of deeper insight, Peter, the husband of the last couple to arrive, tells his wife, Ann, that he has always lived for the future, for something else, rather than for the present. When he cannot tell his wife what he now needs to do, she leaves him to think. His hostess, Elizabeth, with whom he had once had a connection, joins him.

At the climax of the action, Peter and Elizabeth discover that they share a profound communion. They pledge themselves to one another for that instant and forever—but the moment ends when dinner is announced and Ann cannot be found. The guests somewhat drunkenly fear that she has plunged into the sea, but they eventually find her helping in the kitchen. Elizabeth realizes that her moment of happiness is over.

MacLeish believed that women, unlike men, can live in the present. American men, he

Adam Straus's 1995 painting *Descent* calls to mind the enchanted evening spent under a full moon in MacLeish's 1953 play, *This Music Crept by Me Upon the Waters*.

thought, resemble Peter, whom he called the defeated hero of the play. Peter always hopes to better himself but lacks the courage to seize the happiness he pursues. *This Music Crept by Me Upon the Waters* has been staged and was broadcast in Great Britain as a radio play.

Resources

The Library of Congress, which Archibald MacLeish headed from 1939 to 1944, maintains the largest collection of materials by and about him. It includes his notebooks and most of his correspondence. Yale University, where MacLeish studied as an undergraduate, also has a significant collection of related materials. Greenfield Community College, located not far from MacLeish's home in Conway, Massachusetts, has established an archive of the writer's memorabilia, books, and documents.

Archibald MacLeish (1892–1982): A Poem Should Not Mean but Be. This Web site offers a photograph and brief biography of MacLeish, together with links to related sites. (http://web.utk.edu/~jjh6161/IS490/MacLeish.htm)

Academy of American Poets, Poetry Exhibits, Archibald MacLeish. The Academy of American Poets has an informative Web site with a selected bibliography of MacLeish's work, poems and links to other MacLeish sites. (http://www.poets.org/poets/poets.cfm?prmID=48)

A Conversation with Archibald MacLeish. On March 27, 1976, the *Bill Moyers Journal* on the PBS television network broadcast "A Conversation with Archibald MacLeish," and a written transcript of this interview was made. While this interview is apparently unavailable in any currently used video format, the written transcript may be found in the holdings of some libraries and is in the MacLeish Archive at Greenfield Community College.

The Dialogues of Archibald MacLeish and Mark Van Doren. On August 2, 1962, the CBS television network broadcast an hour of the dialogues of MacLeish and the writer and editor Mark Van Doren, which had been filmed on June 18 and 19 of that year. A transcript of these dialogues, together with material not broadcast, is found in *The Dialogues of Archibald MacLeish and Mark Van Doren*, edited by Warren V. Bush and published by E. F. Dutton in 1964.

DAVID W. COLE

Bernard Malamud

BORN: April 26, 1914, Brooklyn, New York
DIED: March 18, 1986, New York, New York
IDENTIFICATION: Novelist and short-story writer who drew upon the Jewish immigrant experience in America for many of his most successful stories.

Bernard Malamud's characteristic works use Jewish American characters and settings yet transcend specific ethnic themes. A blend of fact and fantasy links his stories to universal human problems of survival and moral responsibility. *The Assistant* (1957), which established Malamud's reputation as a major novelist, demonstrated this distinctive style. A poverty-stricken grocery store, not unlike the one Malamud's parents owned in his youth, provides the setting within which a young Italian assistant transforms his original scorn for the aged Jewish grocer into a mythical identification with him and accepts his moral values. Malamud's books won two National Book Awards and a Pulitzer Prize.

The Writer's Life

Bernard Malamud was born in Brooklyn, New York, on April 26, 1914, the eldest of Max Malamud and Bertha Fidelman's two sons. His parents were Russian Jewish immigrants who married after arriving in the United States. His mother, who died when Malamud was fifteen, came from a family that was active in the New York Yiddish theater. His parents operated a small grocery store in the Gravesend section of Brooklyn, a depressed area where few other Jews lived. The store was open sixteen hours a day, and the family occupied a barren apartment above it. Malamud did not remember any books in the house or records or music or even pictures on the walls. When he was nine and confined to bed while convalescing from pneumonia, his father, dipping into the family's meager financial resources, bought him a twenty-volume set of *The Book of Knowledge*. Throughout his childhood, Malamud enjoyed telling stories; some were of his own invention and others retold the plots of movies he had seen.

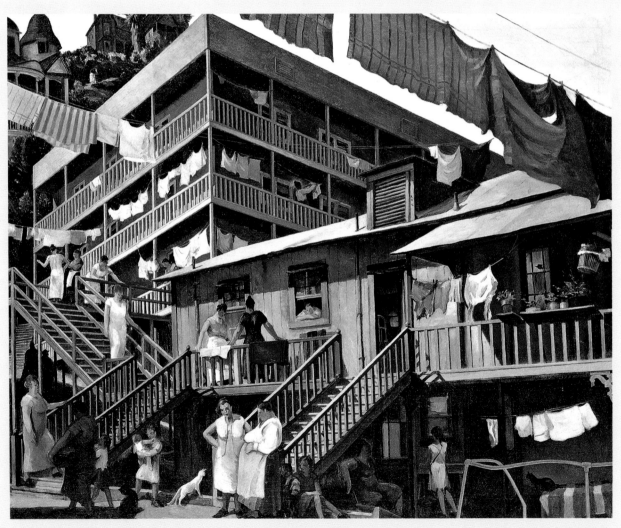

Millard Sheets' 1934 painting *Tenement Flats (Family Flats)* (Smithsonian American Art Museum) depicts an urban neighborhood not unlike the depressed Gravesend section of Brooklyn where Malamud grew up in New York. The son of Russian Jewish immigrants, he lived with his parents and brother above the family's small grocery store.

Education.

Malamud entered Erasmus Hall High School in Brooklyn in 1928. There he earned high grades and praise for his compositions; the school literary magazine also printed his stories. After high school, Malamud chose to enroll in the City College of New York, a tuition-free public college in Manhattan, graduating with a bachelor's degree in 1936. He then attended graduate school at Columbia University for two years but did not receive his master's degree until 1942, after completing his thesis, "Thomas Hardy's Reputation as a Poet in American Periodicals."

Part-Time Writer.

While trying to become a successful author, Malamud was determined to support himself and not become a burden on his family. He sought a civil service position and in 1940 spent a year in Washington, D.C., working for the Census Bureau. From 1940 to 1949 Malamud taught English to recent immigrants at New York City high schools. During this period he wrote many stories, which did not sell, and he completed a novel, "The Light Sleeper," which he later burned because he was dissatisfied with it. In 1945 Malamud married Ann de Chiara, despite his father's objections to her Italian American parentage. The couple had a son, Paul, in 1947, and a daughter, Janna, in 1952.

Malamud believed that college teaching would leave him more time for his writing, so he applied for an English position at Oregon State College. From 1949 to 1961 he made Corvallis, Oregon, his home. Oregon State was essentially an agricultural and technical school—liberal arts departments were referred to as the "lower division." The English department's policy was to reserve literature courses

For years, Malamud supported his family through a series of jobs that included teaching English to night school students and English composition to freshmen at Oregon State University. Throughout this time, he set aside specific days devoted solely to writing.

for members of the faculty holding a doctorate in philosophy degree. Malamud, who had only a master's, was regularly assigned four sections of freshman English composition, paid $3,500 a year, and occasionally earned an extra $100 by teaching an evening short-story workshop for Corvallis residents.

Malamud rigidly structured his time. He reserved Mondays, Wednesdays, and Fridays for teaching classes, holding office hours, and grading papers. He devoted Tuesdays, Thursdays, and Saturdays—and frequently Sundays—to writing. His efforts produced results. In 1950 *Harper's Bazaar*, *Partisan Review*, and *Commentary* each accepted one of

In 1956, Malamud received a Rockefeller grant, which he used to spend a year in Europe. Based in Rome and already married to an Italian American, he learned much about Italian life. Later, he would fill his works with Italian settings and characters.

his short stories; in 1952 his first novel, *The Natural*, appeared. Malamud published three novels and a widely acclaimed volume of short stories during his twelve years at Oregon State.

The college reluctantly granted Malamud a leave of absence in 1956, permitting him to accept a Rockefeller Grant arranged by *Partisan Review*, which he used to spend a year in Europe. Making his headquarters in Rome, Malamud traveled to other countries, absorbing Old World culture. During his stay in Rome, his wife's relatives introduced him to many aspects of Italian life, providing insights that informed his later stories using Italian settings and characters.

Recognition. In 1961 Malamud left Oregon State and joined the faculty of Bennington College, in Bennington, Vermont, where his writing was valued and his teaching schedule

reduced. He taught two courses per semester, and no one seemed concerned if only five or six students registered for his writing classes.

The Assistant earned Malamud many awards and honors. The novel won the Rosenthal Foundation Award of the National Institute of Arts and Letters as well as the Daroff Memorial Fiction Award of the Jewish Book Council of America. It established Malamud's international reputation as an outstanding American author. It was published in England in 1959 and translated into French and German in 1960; it later appeared in fifteen additional languages.

His short-story collection *The Magic Barrel* (1958) won for him a National Book Award for Fiction in 1959 as well as a Ford Foundation Fellowship. In 1964 Malamud was elected to the National Institute of Arts and Letters, and in 1967 he became a member of the American Academy of Arts and Letters. *The Fixer* (1966)

HIGHLIGHTS IN MALAMUD'S LIFE

1914	Bernard Malamud is born in Brooklyn, New York, on April 26.
1928–1932	Attends Erasmus High School, Brooklyn, New York.
1929	His mother, Bertha Fidelman Malamud, dies.
1932	Malamud enters the City College of New York.
1936	Receives bachelor's degree.
1937–1938	Attends Columbia University in New York City.
1940	Works as a clerk in Bureau of the Census, Washington, D.C.
1940–1948	Teaches evening classes at Erasmus Hall High School.
1941	Begins to write short stories.
1942	Awarded master's degree from Columbia University.
1945	Marries Ann de Chiara; moves to Greenwich Village.
1947	Son Paul is born.
1948–1949	Malamud teaches evening classes at Harlem Evening High School.
1949–1961	Serves on English faculty at Oregon State College, Corvallis, Oregon.
1950	Publishes stories in *Harper's Bazaar*, *Partisan Review*, and *Commentary*.
1952	Publishes *The Natural*; father dies; daughter Janna is born.
1956–1957	Malamud lives in Rome and travels in Europe on a *Partisan Review-*Rockefeller grant.
1957	Publishes *The Assistant*.
1958	Publishes *The Magic Barrel*; receives awards for *The Assistant* from the National Institute of Arts and Letters and the Jewish Book Council of America.
1959	Receives National Book Award for *The Magic Barrel*; is awarded a Ford Foundation Fellowship in Humanities and the Arts.
1961	Publishes *A New Life*; joins faculty of Bennington College, Bennington, Vermont.
1963	Travels in England and Italy.
1964	Elected to the National Institute of Arts and Letters.
1965	Travels in the Soviet Union, France, and Spain.
1966	Publishes *The Fixer*.
1966–1968	Visiting lecturer at Harvard University.
1967	Wins Pulitzer Prize and National Book Award for *The Fixer*; is elected to the American Academy of Arts and Letters.
1970	Receives the Governor's Award from the Vermont Council of the Arts.
1983	Receives the Gold Medal for Fiction from the American Academy and Institute of Arts and Letters.
1982	Undergoes heart-artery bypass surgery and suffers a stroke.
1986	Dies of heart attack on March 18.

won both the Pulitzer Prize and the National Book Award for fiction in 1967. Malamud served as a visiting lecturer at Harvard University between 1966 and 1968. In 1983 the American Academy and Institute of Arts and letters awarded him the Gold Medal for Fiction.

Last Years. Malamud published seven novels and five collections of short stories during his lifetime. Although the success of his books relieved him of any need to earn his living through college teaching, Malamud continued as a member of the Bennington faculty. He rejected arguments that teaching interfered with his writing; he did not want to stop doing something he did well and also enjoyed. During the 1960's Malamud gradually reduced his teaching load to one prose fiction class for one term each year. Even after he retired, Malamud continued to teach for a month in the spring and a month in the fall, living in Bennington during the summer and retreating to his New York City apartment in the winter.

After his retirement Malamud's health deteriorated. He underwent heart-artery bypass surgery in 1982, which was followed by a stroke that left him weak and debilitated. He was at work on another novel when he died of a heart attack on March 18, 1986.

Usually too poor to spend money on books, the writer's father dipped into precious savings to purchase the twenty-volume set of *The Book of Knowledge* for Bernard, who was nine years old and recovering from pneumonia.

The Writer's Work

Issues in Malamud's Fiction. Critics often categorize Malamud as a Jewish American writer. Malamud resisted this label because he felt it implied that he was interested only in Jews. He insisted that his work held universal meaning because he used Jews to illustrate major aspects of the human condition. For Malamud, Jews were symbolic of the tragic nature of human experience; Jewish history itself was simply a dramatic version of the fate of all human beings. Malamud argued that he wrote about Jews because he knew them, because he could hear their voices, and because they excited his imagination. The themes he explored—suffering, personal responsibility, and moral obligation—were not limited to the Jewish experience but could be found within all personal experience.

Malamud frequently mixed fantasy and fable beneath the surface realism of his stories. In *The Natural*, Roy Hobbs and his magic bat, Wonderboy, restage on the baseball field the mythic legend of Sir Percival and his quest for the Holy Grail. Some critics expressed discomfort with Malamud's use of fantasy. However, others noted that Malamud's short stories effectively combine flights of fantasy with realistic description and argued that his dream sequences add symbolic weight to his novels.

Malamud's first novel was *The Natural* (1952), a story about a baseball player and his magic bat. Like much of the author's work, it offers a thought-provoking mixture of fantasy and realism. In 1984, *The Natural* was made into a film starring Robert Redford. Unfortunately, the Hollywood happy ending reversed the author's intent.

SOME INSPIRATIONS BEHIND MALAMUD'S WORK

The most important influences on Malamud's work were his parents, especially his father, who practiced a form of secular Judaism that stressed moral rather than creedal aspects of religion. He is clearly the model for the sternly ethical grocer in *The Assistant*. Malamud's parents rarely attended the synagogue and did not maintain a kosher home—both practices would have been difficult, as they lived in an area of Brooklyn where few other Jews resided. They spoke both Yiddish and English at home and took their son to the Yiddish-language theater whenever they could. This exposure provided Malamud with examples of the immigrant English speech that he used so effectively for many of his characters. He credited his father's stories of life in czarist Russia as the inspiration for *The Fixer*, especially the character of Mendel Beiliss, who was accused of ritual murder.

Although much of his best fiction uses urban settings and constricted locations to set the mood, Malamud himself greatly enjoyed living in small towns and rural locations. He used such experiences effectively in two of his novels. The scenic beauty of Oregon provides an ironic contrast to the pettiness of campus affairs in *A New Life*. The affectionate description of the Vermont landscape in *Dubin's Lives* testifies to Malamud's enjoyment of his own life in Bennington.

Malamud credited the films of Charlie Chaplin for teaching him how to cut rapidly from scene to scene as well as for showing him how to mix comedy and sadness in the same story. He claimed that he was more affected by American authors than by the Yiddish and Russian authors—Isaac Bashevis Singer, Fyodor Dostoevski, and Anton Chekhov—with whom he was often compared. He acknowledged the powerful influence of Nathaniel Hawthorne, and commentators have noted the many themes that the two authors share: a stress on morality, the mixing of dream and reality, and ambiguity of characterizations and endings. Malamud's use of immigrant English and Yiddish inflections drew heavily on the oral literary tradition exemplified in the works of Mark Twain.

LIVE AND LET LIVE IN RUSSIA.
"Your money, Jew, or your life!"—*The cry for ages.*

Ethical behavior rather than religious belief is a basic theme of Malamud's work. Inspired by his father's stories of czarist Russia, where Jews were persecuted, the author used Jewish tragedy to relate human tragedy.

People in Malamud's Fiction.

Most of Malamud's characters are American Jews, often of the immigrant generation and frequently poverty-stricken workers or small shopkeepers. Malamud does little with the religious aspects of Judaism, stressing instead the moral values that his characters embrace. In *Dubin's Lives* (1979), for example, specific Jewish themes are not discussed, but Malamud's major character is an American Jew for whom Judaism is marginal to his life.

Italian characters are the second most common ethnic group in Malamud's fiction. He drew on his own observations of people in the neighborhood where he grew up, family and friends whom he met through his wife, and others whom he came to know during his residences in Italy.

Themes in Malamud's Fiction.

The basic theme throughout all of Malamud's work is that of personal and social responsibility, which is generally realized through suffering—often in a prisonlike atmosphere. In *The Natural*, Hobbs cannot master his desire for personal gratification and, as a consequence, fails. In *The Assistant* the claustrophobic grocery store is a constricted environment in which the grocer, Morris Bober, and his assistant, Frank Alpine, are forced to accept responsibility toward each other, thereby achieving self-respect and a measure of personal freedom. Yakov Bok in *The Fixer* is literally imprisoned and forced to undergo torture before arriving at a state of moral grace.

From the 1955 series, *Great Ideas of Western Men,* this painting by George Giusti reflects Malamud's interest in all of humanity. Many of his characters were Jews and Italians, but Malamud always insisted on the universality of their experiences.

Although the Holocaust is rarely dealt with directly in Malamud's work, it resonates throughout his most powerful short stories and novels. Malamud stated that the rise of Adolf Hitler and the events of World War II helped to inspire both his interest in Jewish history and his desire to become a writer. *The Fixer* takes place in czarist Russia long before the Holocaust, but much of the impact of the work is generated by the knowledge of what occurred thirty years later.

Later Work. His winning both the Pulitzer Prize and the National Book Award for *The Fixer* in 1967 marked the high point in critical and public acceptance of Malamud's work. Malamud was hailed as a major American writer, and his novels and short stories were assigned in college and high school literature courses. The novels and short stories that he published after 1967 received less enthusiastic receptions. His last completed novel, *God's Grace* (1982), a fantasy about the world after a nuclear holocaust destroys the human race, mystified many readers. Few thought the posthumous publication of his incomplete *The People: and Other Uncollected Fiction* in 1989 added anything to his reputation.

BIBLIOGRAPHY

Abramson, Edward. *Bernard Malamud Revisited*. New York: Twayne Publishers, 1993.

Astro, Richard, and Jackson J. Benson, eds. *The Fiction of Bernard Malamud*. Corvallis: Oregon State University Press, 1977.

Bilik, Dorothy Seidman. *Immigrant Survivors: Post-Holocaust Consciousness in Recent Jewish Fiction*. Middletown, Conn.: Wesleyan University Press, 1981.

Ducharme, Robert E. *Art and Idea in the Novels of Bernard Malamud: Toward "The Fixer."* The Hague, Netherlands: Mouton, 1974.

Field, Leslie A., and Joyce W. Field, eds. *Bernard Malamud: A Collection of Critical Essays*. Englewood Cliffs, N.J.: Prentice-Hall, 1975.

_____. *Bernard Malamud and the Critics*. New York: New York University Press, 1970.

Helterman, Jeffrey. *Understanding Bernard Malamud*. Columbia: University of South Carolina Press, 1985.

Kosofsky, Rita N. *Bernard Malamud: A Descriptive Bibliography*. Westport, Conn.: Greenwood Press, 1991.

Ochshorn, Kathleen G. *The Heart's Essential Landscape: Bernard Malamud's Hero*. New York: Peter Lang, 1990.

Richman, Sidney. *Bernard Malamud*. New York: Twayne Publishers, 1966.

Roth, Philip. *Reading Myself and Others*. New York: Farrar, Straus and Giroux, 1975.

Salzberg, Joel. *Bernard Malamud: A Reference Guide*. Boston: G. K. Hall, 1985.

Sío-Castiñeira, Begoña. *The Short Stories of Bernard Malamud: In Search of Jewish Post-Immigrant Identity*. New York: Peter Lang, 1998.

LONG FICTION

1952   The Natural
1957   The Assistant
1961   A New Life
1966   The Fixer
1971   The Tenants
1979   Dubin's Lives
1982   God's Grace

SHORT FICTION

1958   The Magic Barrel
1963   Idiots First
1969   Pictures of Fidelman: An Exhibition
1973   Rembrandt's Hat
1983   The Stories of Bernard Malamud

1989   *The People: and Other Uncollected Fiction*
1997   The Complete Stories

NONFICTION

1991   Conversations with Bernard Malamud, ed. Lawrence M. Lasher
1996   Talking Horse: Bernard Malamud on Life and Work, ed. Alan Cheuse and Nicholas Delbanco

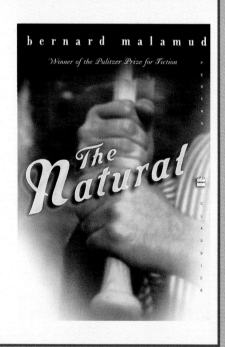

bernard malamud
Winner of the Pulitzer Prize for Fiction
The Natural
PERENNIAL CLASSICS

Reader's Guide to Major Works

THE ASSISTANT

Genre: Novel
Subgenre: Domestic realism
Published: New York, 1957
Time period: 1930's
Setting: Brooklyn, New York

Themes and Issues. Many critics regard *The Assistant* as Bernard Malamud's most successful novel. In it he best integrates his central theme—the transcendent value of redemptive suffering—with the actions of his characters. The grocer, Morris Bober, is unsuccessful financially but is a successful man, because he demonstrates true moral responsibility. His assistant, Frank Alpine, achieves redemption in the course of the novel. The gloomy setting of the failing grocery store in a poverty-stricken neighborhood is described realistically, but it functions symbolically and metaphorically as well. The grocery store is an enclosed world where time stands still and the depression of the 1930s never seems to end, as the characters work out their spiritual destinies.

The Plot. Frank Alpine, an unemployed young Italian, joins another neighborhood tough in robbing Morris Bober's grocery store. The robbery is a fiasco; the grocer had very little money. Frank suffers remorse over his actions and volunteers to work for Bober, who cannot pay him but provides food and shelter. Frank admires Bober's unbending integrity and becomes an apprentice, learning how to operate the store while also striving to emulate the grocer's moral character. Nevertheless, Frank often reverts to his previous behavior, occasionally helping himself to cash from the register and

During the depression of the 1930s, homeless camps like the one shown here appeared throughout urban America. The grocery store in *The Assistant,* the 1957 novel that won Malamud international acclaim, represents the despair of these hard times.

climbing up a dumbwaiter to spy on Bober's daughter, Helen, as she takes a bath.

When Helen shows an interest in him, Frank's feelings for her change from simple lust to love. However, Bober catches Frank stealing cash and orders him out of the store, crushing Frank's hopes for the future. Later Frank sees some toughs attacking Helen and comes to her rescue. Believing he has no further hope with her, he takes advantage of her disheveled state to force himself upon her, earning her hatred.

Eventually, when Bober dies, Frank takes his place, putting on the grocer's apron and dedicating himself to carrying out Bober's dream of sending Helen to college. Associating Bober's moral superiority with being Jewish, Frank has himself circumcised and converts to Judaism.

Analysis. Where *The Natural* describes a moral failure, *The Assistant* dramatizes a moral success. Frank is ultimately initiated into a new spiritual life as he learns sympathy, generosity, and discipline from Bober. The novel makes it clear that although Bober's version of moral responsibility is based on his understanding of Jewish Law, his practices are part of a larger Judeo-Christian tradition. At Bober's funeral the rabbi notes that Bober, though not an observant Jew, lived his life according to Jewish ethical principles. However, those principles are not limited to Judaism. Bober's suffering and sacrifices evoke echoes of the Christian Jesus. Frank's memories are filled with images of St. Francis of Assisi, with whom he identifies as he practices living the way Bober lived.

The gloomy atmosphere of the declining grocery store adds power to the novel, forcing its characters to focus their thoughts and energies inward. Despite the novel's stagnant setting, Malamud's complicated plot keeps the story in continuous motion. The novel is grimly positive in its outlook: Although the store is described as a tomb—an open grave—it is the tomb in which Frank's resurrection occurs.

SOURCES FOR FURTHER STUDY

Freedman, William. "From Bernard Malamud, with Discipline and with Love (*The Assistant* and *The Natural*)." In *Bernard Malamud: A Collection of Critical Essays*, edited by Leslie A. Field and Joyce W. Field. Englewood Cliffs, N.J.: Prentice-Hall, 1975.

Ochshorn, Kathleen G. *The Heart's Essential Landscape: Bernard Malamud's Hero*. New York: Peter Lang, 1990.

Richman, Sidney. *Bernard Malamud*. New York: Twayne Publishers, 1966.

Roth, Philip. *Reading Myself and Others*. New York: Farrar, Straus and Giroux, 1975.

THE FIXER
Genre: Novel
Subgenre: Psychological symbolism
Published: New York, 1966
Time period: 1911–1913
Setting: Kiev, Ukraine

Themes and Issues. Characteristic Malamud themes dominate this novel: the importance of assuming personal responsibility and the value of suffering as a means of achieving moral rectitude. Malamud wished to produce a work dealing with the destructive effect of false accusations based on prejudice and ignorance. He considered fictionalizing the Dreyfus Affair, in which Albert Dreyfus, a captain in the French army, was convicted of treason in 1894, or the Sacco and Vanzetti Case, a highly publicized trial of two Italian immigrant anarchists in Massachusetts who were convicted and executed in 1927 for murdering two bank guards. However, these episodes failed to excite Malamud's imagination. Remembering stories his father had told him about the trial of Mendel Beiliss, who was accused of ritual murder in czarist Russia, he realized that this story could evoke images of the Holocaust.

The Plot. The word *Bok* means "goat" in Yiddish, and Yakov Bok becomes the ultimate scapegoat. Bok is a "fixer," or handyman, whose wife has deserted him. He is unable to earn a living in his small, poverty-stricken Jewish village in the Ukraine. He leaves his rural home to seek a better fortune in the city of Kiev. On a ferry crossing the Dnieper River, he encounters a viciously anti-Semitic boat-

Malamud's novel *The Fixer* (1966) was based on a real story about a Jew falsely accused of murder. Though it takes place in czarist Russia, the events could easily have occurred in Nazi Germany. Alan Bates starred in the 1968 film.

man. In Kiev, he rescues Nicolai Lebedev, a Russian lying helplessly drunk in the street, even though Lebedev is wearing the emblem of an anti-Semitic organization in his lapel. In gratitude Lebedev hires Bok to paint his apartment and then makes him the foreman of his brick factory. Bok, attempting to hide his Jewish identity, lives at the brickworks, which is situated in an area forbidden to Jews.

When a young boy, whom Bok has chased from the brickyard, is found stabbed to death, Bok is charged with his murder and accused of having drained the child's blood to use in baking Passover matzos. Bibikov, the first magistrate to investigate the case, discovers that Bok is a skeptic and a free thinker. He becomes convinced of Bok's innocence. However, the fanatical chief prosecutor believes every word of the accusation and concocts evidence against Bok. When Bibikov is found hanging in the cell next to Bok's, apparently murdered, Bok is placed in solitary confinement in the Kiev jail.

The longest section—more than half the novel—describes Bok's suffering in jail as he is beaten, nearly poisoned, kept chained to the wall, and continually strip-searched. Under constant pressure to confess to the murder, Bok steadfastly refuses, realizing that his confession would be used to justify attacks on the entire Jewish population. During the two years that elapse between Bok's arrest and his trial, he learns to be more accepting of human frailty. He forgives his wife for leaving him and reluctantly accepts his political role. The novel ends with Bok on his way to trial; Malamud leaves the reader to decide whether he will be found guilty or innocent. Reviewers were divided over the question of Bok's fate.

Analysis. *The Fixer* won glowing praise from the majority of critics when it first appeared, and it received both the Pulitzer Prize and National Book Award for fiction in 1967. The few reviewers who found fault with it objected to the lengthy, detailed description of Bok's suffering in prison. For most readers, however, the novel maintains interest by focusing on Bok's inner life: his reactions to his imprisonment and torture and the ways in which he learns to accept responsibility for his life.

The symbolism of the novel has many layers. In part, it recalls the biblical story of Job. When the book begins, Bok rails at God, claiming that when Cossacks attack Jewish villages, God hides in the outhouse. Before the end of the novel, Bok has made his peace with God and has reluctantly accepted his role as a scapegoat. Much of the imagery evokes the story of Jesus. When a guard smuggles in a copy of the Gospels, Bok is fascinated as, for the first time, he reads the life of Jesus. The fanatic hatred of Jews and the inaccurate myths about Jewish practices, accepted on all levels of Russian society, explain Bok's torment and—by implication—the greater tragedy of European Jews in the 1940s. Although the Holocaust is never mentioned, much of the novel's power is generated through the reader's awareness of the parallels between Bok's personal suffering and that of the millions who suffered and died in Nazi death camps.

SOURCES FOR FURTHER STUDY

Friedberg, Maurice. "History and Imagination—Two Views of the Beiliss Case." In *Bernard Malamud and the Critics*, edited by Leslie A. Field and Joyce W. Field. New York: New York University Press, 1970.

Friedman, Alan Warren. "The Hero as Schnook." In *Bernard Malamud and the Critics*, edited by Leslie A. Field and Joyce W. Field. New York: New York University Press, 1970.

Hoag, Gerald. "Malamud's Trial: *The Fixer* and the Critics." In *Bernard Malamud: A Collection of Critical Essays*, edited by Leslie A. Field and Joyce W. Field. Englewood Cliffs, N.J.: Prentice-Hall, 1975.

Ochshorn, Kathleen G. *The Heart's Essential Landscape: Bernard Malamud's Hero*. New York: Peter Lang, 1990.

THE NATURAL

Genre: Novel
Subgenre: Comic epic
Published: New York, 1952
Time period: 1930s
Setting: Chicago, Illinois; New York

Themes and Issues. Although Malamud's first novel is his only book without Jewish characters, it is dominated, nevertheless, by themes similar to those found in his later work. *The Natural* is a baseball novel that also incorporates mythical legends of King Arthur and his Knights of the Round Table, especially that of Sir Percival and the quest for the Holy Grail. The novel's hero, Roy Hobbs, is urged to seek redemption and achieve personal and moral responsibility. Unlike protagonists in *The Assistant* and *The Fixer*, however, Hobbs fails to learn from his experiences, and the consequence is failure.

The Plot. *The Natural* begins with a prologue in which the teenage Hobbs, heading to Chicago for a tryout with the Cubs, is lured by a seductive woman to her hotel room, where she shoots him. The main narrative begins fifteen years later, when a thirty-four year-old Hobbs joins the New York Knights. His ambition is to become the best player ever to enter the game. Using Wonderboy, the baseball bat he carved out of a lightning-struck tree, Hobbs sets hitting records and soon carries the Knights into the thick of a pennant race.

Hobbs becomes sexually involved with Memo Paris, the niece of the Knights' manager Pop Fisher, and soon finds himself falling into a batting slump that threatens disaster for the team. He returns to his magical form when he is asked to hit a home run for a hospitalized young boy who idolizes him. Hobbs becomes attracted to a woman in the stands, Iris Lemon, a thirty-three-year-old grandmother. Although Hobbs finds Iris's love ennobling, he leaves her. He is unable to accept the fact that marrying her would make him a grandfather; he cannot commit to the responsibilities of that role.

Hobbs resumes his affair with Memo. She colludes with gangsters to fix the playoff game between the Knights and the Pirates. Hobbs agrees to throw the game, but he experiences a change of heart and attempts to win. However, it is too late to undo the wrong choices he has made; his magic bat Wonderboy breaks as he attempts to use it, and in the final inning he strikes out. He angrily returns the bribe money and leaves the team and the game of baseball in disgrace.

Analysis. Although the baseball scenes are realistic, the allegorical elements add a supernatural dimension to the story. Hobbs's bat, Wonderboy, clearly represents King Arthur's sword Excalibur, and Coach Pop Fisher evokes images of the mythic Fisher King. However, Malamud's use of the quest for a baseball pennant as the parallel to the search for the Holy Grail transforms the novel into a comic rather than a tragic epic. *The Natural* also alludes to baseball legends: the home run by Babe Ruth to encourage a sick boy and the Chicago White Sox player Shoeless Jackson's throwing of the 1919 World Series in the "Black Sox" scandal. In his relations with the two women, Hobbs undergoes and fails his trial by love. He rejects the spiritual Iris, who urges him to seek redemption by accepting responsibility, and instead chooses the materialistic Memo, who brings him temptation and moral ruin.

Echoing the magic of baseball, Morris Kantor's 1934 painting *Baseball at Night* (Smithsonian American Art Museum, Washington, D. C.) also evokes Malamud's first novel *The Natural*. Though helped by a magical bat, the book's baseball-playing hero is no real hero.

The Natural received little attention when it was first published and did not sell well. After the appearance of Malamud's more successful *The Assistant*, critics reassessed the earlier work and celebrated its virtues. The 1984 film version of *The Natural* starring Robert Redford stimulated popular interest in the novel, and its sales today exceed those of Malamud's other works. However, the movie reversed Malamud's ending: Roy hits a home run in his last turn at bat, instead of striking out, thoroughly subverting Malamud's intended moral.

SOURCES FOR FURTHER STUDY

Abramson, Edward A. *Bernard Malamud Revisited*. New York: Twayne Publishers, 1993.

Helterman, Jeffrey. *Understanding Bernard Malamud*. Columbia: University of South Carolina Press, 1985.

Turner, Frederick W., III. "Myth Inside and Out: *The Natural*." In *Bernard Malamud and the Critics*, edited by Leslie A. Field and Joyce W. Field. New York: New York University Press, 1970.

Wasserman, Earl R. "*The Natural*: World Ceres." In *Bernard Malamud and the Critics*, edited by Leslie A. Field and Joyce W. Field. New York: New York University Press, 1970.

Other Works

DUBIN'S LIVES (1979). This novel's protagonist, William Dubin, is an elderly biographer who finds it difficult to complete the life of D. H. Lawrence that he is writing. The plot involves a May-December romance between Dubin and Fanny Bick, a part-time house cleaner for Dubin and his wife. When Fanny attempts to seduce Dubin in his study, he refuses her advances out of respect for his wife. However, he then arranges a trip to Italy, ostensibly for research on Lawrence, and invites Fanny to join him.

After Fanny runs off with a gondolier in Venice, Dubin goes home. When Fanny returns to Vermont, their affair becomes passionate. Dubin's writing advances, but his relations with his wife and family deteriorate, and he experiences long bouts of depression. In the end, Dubin returns to his wife. In a typical Bernard Malamud ending, the protagonist chooses a life of moral responsibility over a life of passionate fulfillment. To some critics, the novel's ending appeared contrived because the unfolding plot had suggested that Dubin would make a different choice.

GOD'S GRACE (1982). In this fantastic novel, Calvin Cohn is a paleontologist engaged in undersea research who emerges to discover that a nuclear holocaust has destroyed the rest of humankind and a great flood has ruined the civilized world. He lands on an island and finds that a talking chimpanzee and a handful of other apes have also survived. Hoping to create an ideal society, Cohn attempts to teach his new companions human ways. The apes, however, soon begin killing each other and finally slay Cohn. Malamud's combination of science fiction and allegory in this novel confused some reviewers; its comic tone irritated others.

THE MAGIC BARREL (1958). Many critics consider Malamud a master of the short story and praise his work in this medium as much as, if not more than, his novels. When *The Magic Barrel* won the National Book Award for fiction in 1959, it was only the second collection of stories so honored—the first was Nobel laureate William Faulkner's *Collected Stories* (1950).

Malamud's stories, like his novels, reflect his moral concerns. He stresses the need for personal responsibility, the redemptive value of suffering, and the damaging impact of ignorance and prejudice. He frequently dramatizes his ideas by using comic or fantastic plots. "Angel Levine," which served as the basis for both a film and an opera, illustrates this technique. Manischevitz, a tailor whose store has burned down and whose wife is desperately ill, prays to God for help. Shortly thereafter Manischevitz finds a black man in his home who claims to be Alexander Levine, a black Jew and an angel sent by God to help him. Manischevitz does not believe Levine and rejects his aid.

After more disasters, Manischevitz travels to Harlem and visits a synagogue where four black men are discussing the Hebrew Old Testament. He finds Levine drunk in a bar. After reluctantly acknowledging that Levine is an angel, Manischevitz finds his troubles lessening. Similar themes and techniques recur in Malamud's later short-story collections, *Idiots First* (1963), *Pictures of Fidelman: An Exhibition* (1969), and *Rembrandt's Hat* (1973). A volume containing all of Malamud's short stories appeared in 1997 as *The Complete Stories*.

A NEW LIFE (1961). Malamud modeled this social satire about life within a scenic state agricultural college on Oregon State College, where he taught English for twelve years. Expecting to teach at a liberal arts college, S. Levin arrives at Cascadia College only to discover that the humanities are not taught there and that he has been hired to teach endless courses of freshman composition to budding engineers and farmers. The beauty of the physical locale contrasts with the pettiness and intellectual deadness of the

English faculty. Portrayed as a bumbling east-erner and a hapless academic, Levin teaches his first class with his fly unzipped. Outside of class he engages in a series of hilariously unsatisfactory sexual encounters.

In the second half of the novel, Malamud's characteristic theme of the acceptance of moral responsibility through suffering and renunciation emerges. Levin has an affair with the wife of the director of freshman composition. Although Levin's infatuation with her is soon over, he agrees to marry her when she becomes pregnant, taking the woman and her two adopted children away from Cascadia.

THE TENANTS (1971). This novel dramatizes the literary and political tensions between blacks and Jews in the 1960s. Harry Lesser, a Jewish novelist unable to finish the novel he is working on, is the last tenant in a decaying building that the landlord wants to tear down. A squatter, the black writer Willie Spearmint, moves into the building. The two men viciously criticize each other's writings and then clash on racial grounds. After Willie burns Harry's manuscript, Harry destroys Willie's typewriter and then the two tangle physically. The novel did little to enhance Malamud's reputation.

In his social satire *New Life,* Malamud draws upon his twelve years of teaching at Oregon State College, an agricultural and technical school in Corvallis. The book was published in 1961, the year he left Oregon.

Resources

Bernard Malamud donated many of his manuscripts, including typescripts and proofs of *The Natural*, *The Assistant*, *A New Life*, *The Fixer*, *Pictures of Fidelman*, and several of his short stories, to the Library of Congress. Houghton Library at Harvard University holds his letters to John Hawkes. Malamud's letters to Harvey Swados are in the Amherst Library Archives and the manuscript collection of the University of Massachusetts, Amherst. The Berg Collection of the New York Public Library contains his correspondence with Rosemary Beck. Malamud's journals and private letters are in the possession of his family and are not open to the public.

Oregon State University Library. The Bernard Malamud Papers in Special Collections focus primarily on Malamud's years on the faculty from 1949 to 1961 and include letters describing his thoughts and feelings while writing *A New Life*. His colleagues in the English department contributed manuscript letters and clippings in their possession. The library also holds a collection of Malamud first editions. The university hosted conferences examining Malamud's life and work in 1976 and 1996. Papers read at the 1976 conference were published in *The Fiction of Bernard Malamud* (1977), edited by Richard Astro and Jackson L. Benson.

Bernard Malamud Society. The Bernard Malamud Society organized the 1996 conference at Oregon State University. It publishes a newsletter devoted to keeping scholars aware of conferences and new research. For information contact Dr. Evelyn Avery at Towson State University, Towson, MD 21228.

The Unofficial Bernard Malamud Home Pages. This Internet site provides an extensive bibliography as well as a detailed chronology of Malamud's life. (http://www.dokkyo.ac.jp/~esemioo6/malamud)

MILTON BERMAN

David Mamet

BORN: November 30, 1947, Chicago, Illinois
IDENTIFICATION: Late-twentieth-century dramatist, director, producer, and actor, whose plays have been adapted for film and television.

David Mamet began writing plays, some of them adaptations of foreign-language classics, in 1968. In the following decades he branched out into screenwriting, television scripts, radio plays, novels, poetry, nonfiction, and children's literature. His award-winning plays *American Buffalo* (1975) and *Glengarry Glen Ross* (1983) earned distinction for their harsh examinations of frustrated, potentially criminal men—many would call them "losers"—who discover their capacity for immorality during crisis and corrupt circumstances. Mamet is famous for his skillful use of dialogue and infamous for his use of profanity. His recurrent theme of the vicious American business world and his portrayal of inarticulate, tormented characters in conflict have earned him many awards. His plays are frequently revived in repertory theater and studied in college classrooms.

The Writer's Life

David Alan Mamet was born on November 30, 1947, near Chicago, Illinois, and grew up on Chicago's predominantly Jewish South Side. His Russian Jewish parents, Lenore Silver Mamet and Bernard Morris Mamet, were, respectively, a teacher and a labor lawyer.

Childhood. Mamet had a difficult childhood. His parents divorced when he was eleven years of age. His mother married his father's colleague, who was cruel and violent to him, his older sister, Lynn, and his younger brother, Tony. Mamet and his sister helped each other through numerous incidents of mental and physical abuse.

Mamet spent a lot of time with his maternal grandfather, who was from Warsaw, Poland. His grandfather was a salesman whom Mamet admired as a great storyteller.

Introduction to Theater. Mamet enjoyed reading and mimicking the various dialects of Chicago and, as a teenager, wanted to be an actor. He moved into his father's home in Chicago when he was fifteen and started acting in small roles at the Hull House Theatre. Talent was spread among his siblings; Mamet's sister is also a screenwriter, and his brother is a musician and actor.

Mamet studied literature at Goddard College in Vermont, where he and became interested in the works of the Russian dramatist Anton Chekhov. In 1968 and 1969, he studied acting at New York's Neighborhood Playhouse School of Theater.

From Acting to Writing. As an undergraduate, Mamet wrote a comical revue, *Camel*, which was produced in 1968. He realized he was better at writing than acting and created characters from his experiences in various jobs, including washing windows, cleaning offices, driving taxis, and working in factories. Most important to his writing was a hateful job in a real estate agency that required him to sell useless land in the Southwest; he later portrayed the greed and hypocrisy he witnessed there in *Glengarry Glen Ross*.

After college, Mamet returned to Chicago. There he helped to found the St. Nicholas Theater Company, which produced many of his early plays. He believed

Mamet's characters are frequently desperate American businessmen. As reflected in Wade Schuman's painting *Conversation*, they may be good salesmen but they struggle to communicate about the important things in life. The playwright has no such problem, having long been praised for his powerful use of dialogue.

he could more successfully direct young actors if he used his own material. Three early plays, *Duck Variations* (1972), *Sexual Perversity in Chicago* (1974), and *American Buffalo*, were quite successful. When *American Buffalo* earned an Obie (off-Broadway) Award in 1976, Mamet received national recognition.

From Stage to Screen.

A prolific writer, Mamet gained increasing acclaim for a string of plays, including *The Woods* (1977) and the Obie Award–winning *Edmond* (1982). Mamet established himself as a major dramatist of the late twentieth century with two popular and controversial plays: the Pulitzer Prize–winning *Glengarry Glen Ross*, a savage depiction of the American business world, and *Speed-the-Plow* (1988), a stinging examination of the film industry.

Mamet on the set of *Homicide*. Society's moral decay and anti-Semitism are leading themes of this 1991 police thriller and his writing in general.

Although Mamet's plays earned national praise, they also received angry reviews. Many critics called Mamet a misogynist, because his male-dominated dramas occasionally portrayed women unsympathetically. He was denounced as distastefully macho and unnecessarily profane. Audiences, however, both loved and hated his heavy-drinking, cigar-smoking, poker-playing, money-hungry characters who easily slide into crime. Mamet's portrayals of corporate executives driven only by their desire to get rich at the expense of their employees, with the underlying accusation that Americans are brainwashed into unthinking consumerism, made audiences uncomfortable.

However, Mamet had captured Hollywood's attention. He was hired to write the screenplay for a new adaptation of *The Postman Always Rings Twice* (1981), based on the novel by James M. Cain. It was considered an impressive screen debut. Among his other admirable adaptations are *The Verdict* (1982), for which he received an Academy Award nomination, *The Untouchables* (1985), based on the 1960s television series of the same name, and *Vanya on 42nd Street* (1994).

Writer-Turned-Director.

Mamet wrote and directed *House of Games* (1987), a portrait of a psychologist who desires to study the scams and stratagems of confidence men but finds herself corrupted by their underworld version of morality. The twisted, trust-nobody plot made the film a blockbuster.

Mamet also wrote and directed the whimsical comedy *Things Change* (1988) and the police thriller *Homicide* (1991), about a Jewish policeman who grapples with self-loathing arising from the anti-Semitism of his colleagues and neighbors. Mamet gained notoriety with the film version of *Oleanna* (1994), based on his 1992 play about a female student who charges her professor with sexual harassment.

Mamet excels at depicting macho con artists and other seedy male characters. When they do appear, women are usually involved with men in troubled relationships similar to that portrayed in Kathryn Jacobi's 1996 painting *Operatic Duet*.

His most famous adaptation of his own play is *Glengarry Glen Ross*, a 1992 film directed by James Foley.

The Essayist. Mamet began writing autobiographical and nonfiction books in 1986 with *Writing in Restaurants*. Other works, including *Some Freaks* (1989), *On Directing Film* (1991), *The Cabin: Reminiscence and Diversions* (1992), *A Whore's Profession: Notes and Essays* (1994), and *Make-Believe Town: Essays and Remembrances* (1996), are important for their insights into his career, his philosophy on writing and directing, and his opinions on the Hollywood movie industry.

Marriage and Domestic Life. On December 21, 1977, Mamet married the actress Lindsay Crouse, who starred in *House of Games*. The couple had two daughters, Willa and Zosia, before divorcing in 1991. Later that year, Mamet married another actress, Rebecca Pidgeon, who acted in Mamet's films *Homicide*, *The Water Engine* (1992), *Oleanna*, *The Spanish Prisoner* (1997), and *The Winslow Boy* (1999). Pidgeon composed the music for the film version of *Oleanna*. She is a respected pop/folksinger and songwriter and has cowritten songs with Mamet. The two settled in a log cabin without electricity in Vermont with their only child, a daughter named Clara.

A self-made success, Mamet once wrote an essay about his difficulty taking vacations, even with his family. By his own account, his wife coaxed him into a stay at an island resort, but all he could think about was sneaking off to the airport to fly back to the office.

Mamet with his first wife, the actress Lindsay Crouse, with whom he has two daughters, Willa, named after author Willa Cather, and Zosia.

HIGHLIGHTS IN MAMET'S LIFE

1947 David Mamet is born on November 30, 1947, in Chicago, Illinois.

1958 His parents divorce.

1968 Mamet studies acting at New York's Neighborhood Playhouse School of Theater; writes his first play, *Camel*.

1969 Graduates from Goddard College in Vermont; works in theater and in real estate telephone sales.

1970 Works at various jobs and teaches drama at Marlboro College.

1971 Returns to Goddard to teach.

1972 Returns to Chicago.

1973 Founds the St. Nicholas Theater Company in Chicago.

1974 Founds the St. Nicholas Players; becomes faculty member of Illinois Arts Council.

1975 *Sexual Perversity in Chicago* receives the Joseph Jefferson Award for best new Chicago play.

1975 Mamet is visiting lecturer in drama, University of Chicago.

1976 *American Buffalo* receives an Obie Award and the Joseph Jefferson Award.

1976 Mamet begins teaching at Yale University School of Drama.

1977 Marries actress Lindsay Crouse; wins the New York Drama Critics Circle Award for *American Buffalo*; wins a Rockefeller grant.

1978 Named associate director and playwright-in-residence of the Goodman Theatre in Chicago; receives Outer Critics Circle Award for contributions to American theater.

1981 Teaches at New York University; makes screenwriting debut with *The Postman Always Rings Twice*.

1983 Stages *Glengarry Glen Ross* in London; *The Verdict* receives nomination for Academy Award for best adapted screenplay.

1984 *Glengarry Glen Ross* wins the Pulitzer Prize and other awards.

1985 Mamet becomes Associate Director of the New Theatre Company.

1987 Makes his film directorial debut with *House of Games*.

1988 Begins teaching film studies at Columbia University, New York.

1991 Divorces Crouse; marries actress Rebecca Pidgeon.

1994 Creates national controversy with *Oleanna*.

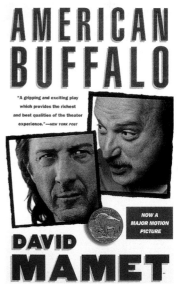

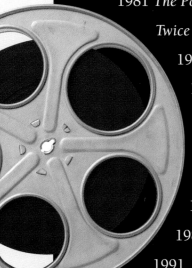

FILMS BASED ON MAMET'S STORIES

The Writer's Work

David Mamet has published plays, scripts, poetry, nonfiction, and children's literature. Prominent qualities in his works are their rapid-action plots, working-class characters, and depictions of the vicious world of business. He frequently portrays con artists to convey the theme that appearances cannot be trusted. Mamet's dialogue is uniquely powerful. His smooth-talking tricksters are eloquent, but otherwise his dialogue features incomplete sentences, the absence of verbs, repetitions, interruptions, and profanity.

Inarticulate speech and obscenities reflect his characters' inability to express themselves. Broken speech represents the breakdown of communication. Communication is crucial to Mamet, because understanding is essential to happiness.

Issues in Mamet's Work. Mamet is a cynic who dramatizes human nature as a mess of greed, troubled relationships, and untrustworthiness. He criticizes businessmen, parents, teachers who abuse their power over others, and con artists who prey on ordinary citizens. Mamet writes con-game thrillers because he sees American commerce as a giant scam. He is alarmed by American consumerism, believing that people will do anything to get rich and will blindly accept anything advertisers tell them.

Mamet's plays deal with survival, whether in school, business, or at home. His characters learn, through violence or trickery, to triumph—or die. This theme was most explicit in the film *The Edge* (1997), in which a good man must resist the attacks of both a homicidal rival for his wife and a powerful grizzly bear, who stalks the men with almost supernatural persistence in the Alaskan wilderness.

Sexual Perversity in Chicago (1974) won Mamet the Joseph Jefferson Award for best new Chicago play in 1975.

Although Mamet's rapidly paced works are often comic, many are tragedies. *Glengarry Glen Ross* is a lose-lose situation for everyone involved, as is *Oleanna*. *The Cryptogram* (1995) is a sad portrait of a family disintegrating because of deceptions. Friendships are lost and relationships broken because of miscommunication.

People in Mamet's Work.

Mamet creates a variety of characters—swindlers, millionaires, elderly Jews, lesbians, inventors—but his most discussed characters are seedy, macho, psychologically twisted men. These tormented, insecure, dehumanized, tough-talking but vulnerable characters are continually chasing the American Dream but are incapable of achieving it.

Mamet's villains manipulate, prey upon, and even destroy the lives of others. Critics describe his works in the language of warfare, saying that he uses words like weapons to display cut-throat ethics.

The Theme of Moral Decay.

Mamet portrays the corruption of the American Dream. In his view, American society no longer values education, upward striving, and individuality but has become instead a place to make quick money.

Mamet blames those in power who spread the myth of equality while brainwashing Americans into thoughtless consumption and suspicion of foreigners. Power at every level corrupts the nation: Parents spank children, and teachers humiliate students, pretending that their intentions are good. However, cruelty is contagious.

Mamet sees the American economy as based on waste, heartless immigration policies, and indifference to international humanitarian causes, all symptoms of moral rot. Embedded in his anger is his Jewish heritage and the hatefulness of anti-Semitism. Mamet portrays characters of varying ethnicities in his dramas so that wider audiences can recognize themselves and perceive the value of cultural differences.

In *Oleanna* Mamet identifies the lack of communication or miscommunication as a key source of conflict between the sexes. William Beckman's 1999 *Overcoats (American Modern)* conveys a similar message.

Mamet and Film.

Mamet is rare in that he had found fame as a dramatist, a screenwriter, and a director. He has directed seven of his screenplays: *House of Games*, *Things Change*, *Homicide*, *Oleanna*, *The Spanish Prisoner*, *The Winslow Boy*, and *State and Main* (2000). He produced *Lip Service* (1988), *A Life in the Theater* (1993), and *Lansky* (1999) for television. Mamet has also acted in films, including *Black Widow* (1986) and *The Water Engine*. He appeared in the documentaries *Sanford Meisner: The American Theatre's Best Kept Secret* (1984) and *Yiddish Cinema* (1991).

Mamet's Literary Legacy.

Mamet is an eminent twentieth-century playwright. Although he has earned a reputation for writing about macho subjects such as crime, poker, and auto racing, he does not write only for men. His smart, frightening, and sometimes infuriating plays satirize his generation and American society in entertaining and original ways.

Mamet has influenced a generation of screenwriters and playwrights, from Eric Bogosian to Quentin Tarantino. The male-dominated casts and staccato dialogue of such writers owe a debt to Mamet. Mamet's influence appears also in the increasingly common portrayal of antiheroic social deviants in film.

BIBLIOGRAPHY

Brewer, Gay. *David Mamet and Film: Illusion/Disillusion in a Wounded Land.* Jefferson, N.C.: McFarland, 1993.

Carroll, Dennis. *David Mamet.* New York: St. Martin's Press, 1987.

Dean, Anne. *David Mamet: Language as Dramatic Action.* Rutherford, N.J.: Fairleigh Dickinson University Press, 1990.

Jones, Nesta, and Steven Dykes, eds. *File on Mamet.* London: Methuen, 1991.

Kane, Leslie, ed. *David Mamet: A Casebook.* New York: Garland, 1992.

_____. *Weasels and Wisemen: Ethics and Ethnicity in the Work of David Mamet.* New York: St. Martin's Press, 1999.

Kolin, Philip, and Colby Kullman, eds. *Speaking on Stage: Interviews with Contemporary American Playwrights.* Tuscaloosa: University of Alabama Press, 1996.

McDonough, Carla. *Staging Masculinity: Male Identity in Contemporary American Drama.* Jefferson, N.C.: McFarland, 1997.

McNaughton, Howard. "Mamet, David (Alan)." In *Contemporary Dramatists.* London: St. James Press, 1999.

Roudané, Matthew. "David Mamet." In *Critical Survey of Drama,* edited by Frank N. Magill. Rev. ed. Vol. 4. Pasadena, Calif.: Salem Press, 1994.

SELECTED PLAYS

1968 Camel
1970 Lakeboat (revised in 1980)
1972 Duck Variations
1974 Sexual Perversity in Chicago
1975 American Buffalo
1976 Reunion
1977 A Life in the Theatre
1977 The Revenge of the Space Pandas
1977 The Water Engine
1977 The Woods
1981 Donny March
1982 Edmond
1983 The Disappearance of the Jews
1983 Glengarry Glen Ross
1984 The Frog Prince
1985 Goldberg Street: Short Plays and Monologues
1986 The Cherry Orchard (adaptation of Anton Chekhov's play)
1987 Three Jewish Plays
1988 Speed-the-Plow
1988 Uncle Vanya (adaptation of Chekhov play)
1990 Three Sisters (adaptation of Chekhov play)
1992 Oleanna
1994 A Life with No Joy in It, and Other Plays and Pieces
1994 No One Will Be Immune, and Other Plays and Pieces
1995 The Cryptogram
1998 The Old Neighborhood: Three Plays
1998 The Spanish Prisoner
1998 The Winslow Boy

SCREENPLAYS

1981 The Postman Always Rings Twice (adaptation of James M. Cain's novel)

1982 The Verdict (based on Barry Reed's novel)
1985 The Untouchables
1987 House of Games
1988 Things Change
1989 We're No Angels
1991 Homicide
1992 Glengarry Glen Ross
1992 Hoffa
1994 Oleanna
1994 Vanya on 42nd Street
1996 American Buffalo
1997 The Edge
1997 The Spanish Prisoner
1997 Wag the Dog (with Hilary Henkin)
1998 Ronin (as Richard Weisz)
1999 The Winslow Boy
2000 State and Main

TELEPLAYS

1988 Lip Service
1990 Five Television Plays
1992 The Water Engine
1993 A Life in the Theater
1999 Lansky

RADIO PLAYS

1978 Prairie du Chien
1985 Cross Patch
1985 Goldberg Street
1989 Dintenfass

LONG FICTION

1994 The Village
1997 The Old Religion
2000 Wilson

POETRY

1990 The Hero Pony
1999 The Chinaman

NONFICTION

1986 Writing in Restaurants
1989 Some Freaks

1989 Donald Sultan: Playing Cards (with Ricky Jay)
1991 On Directing Film
1992 The Cabin: Reminiscence and Diversions
1994 A Whore's Profession: Notes and Essays
1996 Make-Believe Town: Essays and Remembrances
1997 True and False: Heresy and Common Sense for the Actor
1998 Three Uses of the Knife: On the Nature and Purpose of Drama
1999 Jafsie and John Henry: Essays on Hollywood, Bad Boys, and Six Hours of Perfect Poker

CHILDREN'S LITERATURE

1986 Three Children's Plays
1987 The Owl
1988 Warm and Cold (with Donald Sultan)
1995 Passover
1996 The Duck and the Goat
1999 Bar Mitzvah
1999 Henrietta

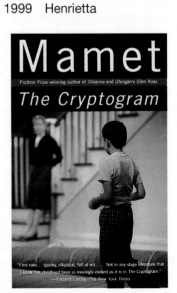

Mamet

Pulitzer Prize-winning author of *Oleanna* and *Glengarry Glen Ross*

The Cryptogram

"First-rate...spooky, elliptical, full of wit.... Not in any stage literature that I know has childhood been as movingly evoked as it is in *The Cryptogram*."
—Vincent Canby, *The New York Times*

Reader's Guide to Major Works

AMERICAN BUFFALO

Genre: Drama
Subgenre: Social criticism, tragicomedy
Produced: New York, 1975
Time period: 1970s
Setting: Chicago, Illinois

Themes and Issues. The rare buffalo-head nickel for which the play is named is symbolic. Like the American buffalo, the three characters of the play are endangered—by their marginal position in the recessed economic era of the 1970s, by their ability to talk loudly enough to drown out their own consciences, by their own ignorance.

The three men spend the entire play in a junk shop planning a burglary. The setting represents both the corruption of their un-derworld-tainted morality and Mamet's idea of American business. Mamet implies that modern businesspeople, which these three are pleased to call themselves, are so bereft of humanitarian values that they merely buy and sell junk, caring only about profits. It is ironic that his characters are plotting to steal what boils down to a handful of change. At last the would-be thieves turn on each other, and their hopes for overnight wealth collapse into inaction, inertia, and ultimately, violence.

The Plot. Don Dubro, the proprietor of an inner-city junk shop, hopes one day to strike it rich. The teenage Bobby, who runs errands for Don, is sent to watch a customer who bought a rare buffalo-head nickel for what Don de-

Dennis Frans (left) and Sean Nelson are seen here in the 1996 film adaptation of *American Buffalo,* for which Mamet won national recognition as well as an Obie and the New York Drama Critics Circle Award for best American play.

cides was too low a price. Their low-life acquaintance Teach soon figures out what the two are quietly and cryptically discussing and weasels his way into the scheme. He thinks the three should break into the customer's house and steal his entire coin collection. Although none of the men know anything about the customer, the coin, or any collection he might have, they plan a robbery for that night.

Teach argues that he should be the burglar because Bobby is too inexperienced; actually, Teach wants as much of the loot as he can get.

For hours, while Bobby comes and goes, Don and Teach argue over details of the plan. Teach also gives several nearly incoherent lectures on the American Dream of free enterprise and on the values of friendship and business. Teach's irritation grows as time passes, partly out of jealousy over Don's concern for Bobby's welfare, and at last his temper explodes. He tears up the shop and assaults Bobby. In the end, they give up on stealing the coin collection, which might not even exist, and take Bobby to the hospital.

SOME INSPIRATIONS BEHIND MAMET'S WORK

Mamet's troubled childhood influenced many of his plays. However, he prefers to speak of teachers and other writers as inspirations. As a student, he read and admired the novels of Willa Cather and Theodore Dreiser, whose works pessimistically critique American society. Sanford Meisner, an important drama teacher and theorist, had a great impact on Mamet's college education. Mamet has adapted works by his favorite playwright, Anton Chekhov, enlivening them with contemporary language.

Mamet has been influenced by the dramatists John Osborne, Harold Pinter, and Samuel Beckett, known for their use of anger and profanity and for their portrayals of victims terrorized by sinister unknown forces. Pinter and Beckett are noted for the dramatic pauses in their works—silences that suggest an inability to communicate. Mamet has also admired the work of the playwright Tennessee Williams, who likewise portrays ordinary, kind people caught in cruel times.

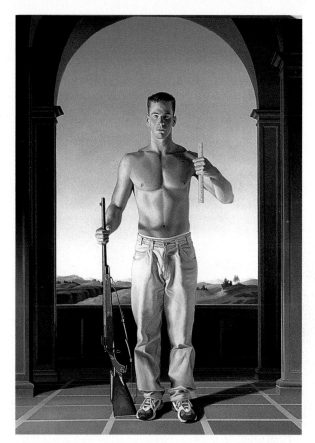

American Rudder (1999) by Wes Hempel. A child of divorce and abuse, Mamet took refuge in reading and listening to his storytelling grandfather. A wide variety of writers from Theodore Dreiser to Anton Chekhov helped steer him to where he is today. He in turn has influenced an entire generation of screenwriters, especially with his focus on alienated males.

The dark humor of *American Buffalo* is a scathing indictment of American business, and its characters find themselves in as much danger as the American Indian and buffalo depicted here in Paul Giovanopoulos's 1995 painting *Buffalo Nickel*.

Analysis. This angry and suspenseful play, which won both Obie and New York Drama Critics Circle Awards for best American play in 1976, is a satire of business ethics and "honor among thieves"—in other words, impulsivity and untrustworthiness. Don and Teach, trapped in aimless, meaningless lives, use language, especially clichés and curses, to goad each other into a "get-rich-quick" scheme. The restriction of the action to a junk shop creates a claustrophobic sense of how limited the men's lives and opportunities are.

Various small incidents, such as phone calls, quarrels, and mysterious and deceitful messages from Bobby, prevent Teach from actually setting out to do the job. These incidents contribute to the humor of the play,

which is funny in a sad and dark way. The characters' language signals that the plan will be frustrated. They interrupt each other, they break off sentences, they swear, they talk loudly about vague concepts, and they never relax from their macho stances to offer sincere words of loyalty and friendship. Because they cannot communicate, they cannot form real relationships—just as the captains of industry never form heartfelt relationships with the consumers of their products.

SOURCES FOR FURTHER STUDY

Barbera, J. V. "Ethical Perversity in America: Some Observations on David Mamet's *American Buffalo*." *Modern Drama* 24, no. 3 (September 1981): 270–275.

Dean, Anne. *David Mamet: Language as Dramatic Action.* Rutherford, N.J.: Fairleigh Dickinson University Press, 1990.

Shipley, Joseph T. "*American Buffalo,* etc." *The Crown Guide to the World's Great Plays: From Ancient Greece to Modern Times.* Rev. ed. New York: Crown, 1984.

GLENGARRY GLEN ROSS

Genre: Play
Subgenre: Social criticism
Produced: New York, 1983
Time period: 1980s
Setting: Seattle, Washington

Themes and Issues. Although the title suggests the rolling hills of Scotland, the real estate agents of this Pulitzer Prize–winning play are actually involved in selling Florida swampland to elderly pensioners. The five characters who work in the agency office are a few rungs up the social ladder from those of *American Buffalo*, but they suffer the same failings. Their jobs require them to practice deceit and fraud on a daily basis. Finding no love in their work or loyalty to the heartless corporate executives, they have bought into the idea that competition is more important than happiness, and their lives are spiritually empty.

Mamet's message is quite clear. Business is oppressive and dehumanizing. It is built on illusion and enslaves both employees and the public. The concern of business is purely money. Business is conducted in the arena of imprisoning offices, where slogans about teamwork conceal the back-stabbing competition. As the play progresses, the characters become like animals—sneaky rats, snarling wolves, or slavering jackals.

The Plot. Four real estate agents are told by the management that the stakes of their monthly sales contest have increased: The two

The venerated actor Jack Lemmon is a desperate real estate agent trying to sell swampland to pensioners in *Glengarry Glen Ross* (1983). The play earned Mamet a Pulitzer Prize in 1984.

Laden with obscenities, the language of *Glengarry Glen Ross* matches the savagery of the business practices it is portraying and the heartlessness of the salesmen. Al Pacino (right) and Kevin Spacey starred in the 1992 film.

among the four who earn the least money will be fired. The news is meant to motivate them; instead, the men become desperate. They receive no sympathy from Williamson, the office manager, who guards the coveted Glengarry leads, the clients who are likely to agree to buy.

Roma seems the most likely to win; he is still smooth and good at the hard sell. Moss plans another way to win: steal the leads, sell them to a rival for a good price, and say good-bye to the heard-hearted executives. Because he knows he would be the first to be suspected, he urges Aaronow, who is on a major losing streak, to commit the burglary. Levene, once the top salesman, now faces unemployment and poverty.

When the leads are found to be stolen the next day, the police come in to interrogate everyone. The identity of the criminal is revealed in a surprise ending that is not really so surprising, considering that all four men had motives and nothing to lose.

Analysis. *Glengarry Glen Ross* is a savage satire about late-twentieth-century business practices. While some critics shrank from the obscenities that pepper the dialogue, most praised the play for its two most important qualities: its anticorporation theme and its brilliant use of language.

A salesman, after all, makes his living with his language. Levene, Moss, Aronow, and Roma each have their individual styles of sales patter and of charming potential clients. They are also capable of menacing and explosive repartee with each other. When Moss and Aaronow discuss stealing the leads, they speak theoretically, with neither man saying exactly what is on his mind. When Levene begs Williamson for the leads, he speaks of his past glories, of his family, of dignity and integrity, unaware that he is humiliating himself in his failure to keep up with changing times and rules. With one another, the salesmen conceal their vulnerability and fears of failure—not to mention their barren consciences and fraudulent jobs—by cursing about bad tips, long hours, bad luck, and their deadbeat customers. Ultimately, their endless talk is intended only to forestall their inevitable doom.

SOURCES FOR FURTHER STUDY

Barnes, Clive, ed. *Best American Plays: Ninth Series, 1983–1992.* New York: Crown Publishers, 1993.

Kane, Leslie, ed. *David Mamet's "Glengarry Glen Ross": Text and Performance.* New York: Garland, 1996.

Kaufman, Stanley. "Deaths of Salesmen." *The New Republic* (October 26, 1992).

THE SPANISH PRISONER

Genre: Screenplay
Subgenre: Suspense/thriller
Released: 1998
Time period: Late 1990s
Setting: Tropical island; New York City

Themes and Issues. All the trademark Mamet themes and techniques come together in this

Another of Mamet's plays that was made into a film in 1997, *The Spanish Prisoner* found the comedian Steve Martin (here seen with Campbell Scott) in an anything but comedic role. A sinister study of betrayal, it is the most important film that Mamet both wrote and directed.

film about a young inventor whose work has been stolen by con artists: keen, circuitous dialogue, a crafty plot based on a scam, and suspense rising to a violent surprise ending. Some critics consider Mamet's *The Spanish Prisoner* better than his 1987 con-game thriller, *House of Games*. Some consider it inferior. All, however, agree that *The Spanish Prisoner* is the most important film that Mamet both wrote and directed.

A young man who has invented a priceless formula finds himself targeted by at least one con artist and soon learns that some people are willing to commit murder in order to steal his work. Both the con men and the captains of capitalism are inhumanly greedy, and absolutely nobody can be trusted to be what they appear.

The Plot. Joe Ross, a researcher at a nameless company, has developed an economic formula called the "process," which will allow the com-

pany executives to dominate the world market. On a tropical island, he meets with these executives; he also becomes acquainted with his new secretary, Susan, and with a millionaire named Jimmy Dell. When the company group returns to New York, Dell persuades Joe to carry a package for Dell's sister, who lives there.

Susan continually warns Joe that "you never know who anybody is," but he is flattered by the attentions of Dell, who invites Joe to dinner to meet his pretty sister. Dell advises Joe that he should consult a lawyer about the nature of his obligations to the company and his ownership of the process. As Joe sets out to meet Dell's lawyer, he discovers that the single book containing his process has been switched with a similar-looking, but empty, book. Then he learns that Dell's sister does not exist. He seeks revenge but soon feels like a rat trapped in a maze. Basically a trusting fellow, Joe realizes that everyone is out to get him, and every plea for help from a friend results in betrayal.

Analysis. *The Spanish Prisoner* is about surface appearances and the art of the con. The audience as well as Joe is baffled by what is actually seen and what is only assumed. For example, when the executives ask Joe how much they will earn from the process, he writes a figure on a chalkboard, but the audience does not see what he has written. That which is not seen, like the con artist's stealthy maneuvering, is dangerous. When Joe says, "The process," and after a pause continues, "and by means of the process, to control the world market," it is a typical example of Mamet's dialogue: incomplete, vague, sinister, and therefore, powerful.

Mamet's interest in the strange relationships into which people enter becomes in this film a study of betrayal. The con artist knows the ways in which the world secretly works. Life is a constant series of transactions in which someone is always victimized. Mamet's portrayal of the characters covers a range of emotions and motives—romance, greed, pride, anger and humiliation of the victim—all of which underlie his recurrent themes of misplaced faith and disloyalty, dog-eat-dog capitalism, gamesmanship, and the vanity of human desire.

SOURCES FOR FURTHER STUDY

Bowman, James. "*The Spanish Prisoner.*" *The American Spectator* 31, no. 6 (June 1998): 66–67.

Corliss, Richard. "Trickster David Mamet Beguiles with *The Spanish Prisoner.*" *Time* 151, no. 13 (April 16, 1998): 72.

Fuller, Graham. "April's Favorite Fooler: Interview with David Mamet." *Interview* 28, no. 4 (April 1998): 66.

Other Works

THE CRYPTOGRAM (1995). This Obie Award–winning play, set in 1959, is a bleak autobiographical view of the loss of childhood innocence. Ten-year-old John waits up for his father to come home so they can go on a camping trip. Meanwhile, his mother, Donny, and her friend, Del, have a conversation that gradually turns sinister and horrifying.

Donny, while begging Del to reveal where her husband is, tries to shelter John from the truth that his father is not coming home. She gives him cough syrup to help him sleep; she bribes him with empty promises; she lies. John, in turn, plays stalling games to get attention. His insomnia is one of the play's many frustrations. John intuits that the adults are speaking about their vulnerabilities with evasions and lies in a coded language that he cannot comprehend. He asks endless questions about his father, about death, and about his mother's reactions to some strange objects—a broken teapot, a photograph, a torn blanket, and a large knife.

These clues slowly, though not entirely, illuminate the mystery of the father's whereabouts, of

Charles Ray's 1995 painting *Puzzle Bottle* (Whitney Museum of American Art, New York) echoes the terrible confusion and helplessness felt by ten-year-old John in Mamet's autobiographical and Obie Award–winning play *The Cryptogram* (1995).

the relationship between Donny and Del, of the possibility of murder. Many of John's speeches are macabre, obsessing on death and ghosts. As the family's psychological fabric tatters, the characters vent their rage on one another.

The Cryptogram explores David Mamet's familiar theme of the inability to communicate, here in a domestic setting. John's deepening confusion and fear over a vaguely perceived but intensifying family tragedy dramatize what happens when parents pass their hatred onto their children, whose inexperience makes their terrors psychologically devastating. As Donny tells John, "Things occur. In our lives. And the meaning of them . . . the meaning of them . . . is not clear." The fragmented sentence symbolizes Donny's own fear and uncertainty as well as the universal struggle to decipher the cryptogram of life.

OLEANNA (1992). A college professor, John, is confronted by a student, Carol, who is failing his course. Instead of giving her conventional advice, the professor explains his philosophy of education. He questions whether a college education is valuable and says that Carol's taking notes in class is meaningless if she does not understand his lectures. She cries that nothing he says makes any sense to her. Their conversation is filled with telephone interruptions.

Act 2 reveals that Carol has filed a protest accusing John of sexual harassment based on statements and physical behavior that she found offensive. The conflict is that these actions can be seen as completely innocent, as John claims, or as sexist. Supported by an unidentified group, Carol is no longer nervous and uncertain. As her confidence grows, the professor's evaporates. He will lose his tenure, his career, and his wife, as well as the house they were planning to buy. He absolutely cannot accept these losses.

In act 3 John tries once more to defuse the situation, and the results are shattering. Carol tells him that she has filed new charges of rape but will withdraw both accusations if he changes his ways and allows his own textbook

The actor William H. Macy and the director's wife, Rebecca Pidgeon, appear on stage in a scene from *Oleanna* (1992), in which Mamet takes the war of the sexes to the extreme.

to be banned from campus. John considers such censorship intolerable.

Ultimately, the question in *Oleanna* is not whether sexual harassment has occurred but rather who is persecuting whom. Both characters, relying on the university's policies, have resources to draw upon, but they also have many weaknesses. Carol finds John authoritarian, but his intentions were sympathetic; she undermines his authority by finding him guilty of political incorrectness. The play grows increasingly intense and frightening, erupting from sanity and reason into primal emotion. The enlightening value of *Oleanna* is its demonstration of how men and women can view the same events from entirely different perspectives.

THREE CHILDREN'S PLAYS (1986). This volume contains three whimsical plays that entertain preteens. At the same time, their jokes delight older audiences. The first play, *The Poet and the Rent*, deals with an unemployed young man who cannot sell his poetry. The poet owes the landlord sixty dollars, and through a series of misadventures full of puns and slapstick, he manages several times to gain and lose sixty dollars.

The Revenge of the Space Pandas is a science-fiction tale about a child genius who invents a two-speed clock that transports him, a friend, and his pet talking sheep to a strange planet. There they unintentionally anger the supreme ruler and must escape "death by pumpkin-whacking."

The most powerful of the three plays is *The Frog Prince*. Soon after the Prince is turned into a frog by a witch, his fiancé marries another man. Abandoned in the wilderness, the frog has only his loyal Servingman and a sweet Milkmaid as friends. The Prince attempts several comical ruses to get the Milkmaid to kiss him. When at last he becomes human again, he is no longer arrogantly self-absorbed and has learned much about love and friendship.

Resources

There are no collected archives of David Mamet's manuscripts and papers. Other sources of interest for students of Mamet include the following:

David Mamet Society. Based at the University of Nevada at Las Vegas, the society publishes an annual journal, *The David Mamet Review* (1994), which includes essays and news of Mamet's activities.

Video Recordings. Many video recordings are available featuring Mamet's work or commentary. In *The Playwright Directs: With David Mamet* (1997), produced by Creative Arts Television, Mamet, Lindsay Crouse, and members of the Circle Repertory Company use excerpts from *Dark Pony* (1977) and *Reunion* (1976) to show Mamet directing his own works. *David Mamet* (1985), produced by London Weekend Television and RM Arts, features Mamet himself, discussing his background, his techniques, and his view of the United States as a country headed for self-destruction. In *Emerging Playwrights, Part V: David Mamet* (1993), produced, directed, and edited by Bruce Goldfaden and released by the New York State Education Department's Bureau of Mass Communications, members of the Acting Company discuss Mamet's works.

David Mamet Info Page. This Web site is a comprehensive site, with much information on Mamet's life and works. (http://www.mindspring.com/~jason-charnick/mamet.html)

The Salon Interview. Richard Covington provides an overview of Mamet's career, and a 1997 interview featuring Mamet's views on theater, being Jewish, and mass entertainment media. (http://www.salon.com/music/feature/1997/10/cov_si_24mamet.html)

FIONA KELLEGHAN

Edgar Lee Masters

BORN: August 23, 1868, Garnett, Kansas
DIED: March 5, 1950, Melrose Park, Pennsylvania
IDENTIFICATION: Early twentieth-century Illinois writer who articu-
lated the complex realities of life in a small midwestern town.

Although Edgar Lee Masters wrote fifty books on such diverse topics as
American history, law, and literature, he is most remembered for only two:
Spoon River Anthology (1915) and *The New Spoon River* (1924). In these two
volumes of poetry, deceased residents of Spoon River buried in the fictional
town's cemetery recite short poems in which they describe their perceptions
of life in their central Illinois town. The poetic skill and diversity of voices in
these two collections overshadowed all of Masters's other work, including his
autobiography, *Across Spoon River* (1936), and his biography of Abraham
Lincoln, *Lincoln: The Man* (1931).

The Writer's Life

Edgar Lee Masters was born on August 23, 1868, in Garnett, Kansas, the first of four children born to Emma Jerusha Masters and Hardin W. Masters. His father, a lawyer, had moved to Kansas to start a law firm but could not attract enough clients there. Before Masters was a year old, the family returned to central Illinois and lived in the towns of Petersburg and Lewistown. In his 1936 autobiography, *Across Spoon River*, Masters describes in great detail his parents' loveless marriage and his belief that they were both selfish people who were uncaring toward their four children. Masters later repeated his parents' mistakes, alienating his own children.

Childhood. In Masters's autobiography, which is the main source of information on his early years, he criticizes both his parents: his mother because she was overweight and a bad cook; his father because he did not earn enough money to support his children generously. Even in his later years, the younger Masters seemed oblivious to the effect of his arrogance and insensitivity on other people, with the notable exception of his law clients.

A traumatic event in Masters's childhood was the death of his favorite sibling, Alexander, at the age of five in 1878. Masters never really got over this loss. In his autobiography, written almost six decades after Alexander's death, he vividly describes the profound depression that he and other family members experienced during Alexander's funeral and burial.

Education. Masters attended local Illinois schools and graduated from Petersburg High School in 1889. While in high school, he became a voracious reader, and his interest in both classical and modern literatures continued throughout his life. He attended Knox College in Galesburg, Illinois, for the 1889–1890 acad-

Though critical of his parents, Masters loved and forever mourned the loss of his five-year-old brother. Many years later, he would vividly describe the pain he felt attending Alexander's funeral, evoked here in Eric Fischl's 1980 oil painting *The Funeral.*

emic year, where he studied mostly German, Latin, and Greek. At that time, one could become a lawyer simply by studying law with a lawyer and then passing the bar exam. In 1890 and 1891, Masters studied law in his father's law office and was admitted to the Illinois Bar in 1891. He practiced law with his father from 1891 to 1892, but the clear animosity between the two men soon put an end to their partnership. From 1892 to 1920 Masters had a successful law practice in Chicago; he was a partner of the famous American lawyer Clarence Darrow from 1903 to 1911.

Legal Success. Masters's autobiography describes at great length many cases in which he was involved during his twenty-nine years of law practice. In an important 1914 case he represented a waitresses' union in Chicago, that the restaurant owners' association had attempted to destroy through intimidation. Although full protection for unionized workers would not be approved by the federal government until the presidency of Franklin D. Roosevelt over two decades later, Masters attempted in this case to set some limits on the power employers have over their employees. Masters's case was unsuccessful, but it paved the way for future cases in which employers were held liable for violations of employees' constitutional rights.

Masters often represented people who had been exploited by wealthier individuals. In the mid-1890s, he represented elderly Polish immigrants who had been defrauded by a land developer named Ullman. The Receks did not speak English, and Ullman had persuaded them to trade their valuable lot in Chicago for a building encumbered with numerous liens. He assured them in his contract that he had clear and full title to this building, but he never told

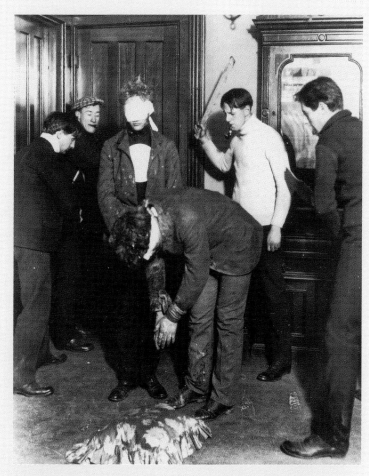

Masters briefly attended Knox College in Galesburg, Illinois, where he acquired a lifelong respect for German, Latin, and Greek. He left to study law, which he practiced for twenty-nine years, often on behalf of the exploited. Shown here is a Knox College fraternity initiation.

them about the liens. Masters sued Ullman, and eventually the property was returned to the Receks, with a large punitive judgment against Ullman. Masters argued the case as a contract case and persuaded the jury and the appellate judges that Ullman's fraud and deception had violated the rights of the Receks.

In another case, Masters represented a minor named Helen Lee. In the presence of a lawyer and witnesses, Lee's dying mother had signed an agreement with her brother, Thomas Bermingham, and his wife that the couple would raise Lee and hold for her the entire estate, which amounted to almost $300,000. The contract was signed by Lee's mother, the Berminghams, and the required number of witnesses. Thomas Bermingham died shortly after his sister, and his widow, who then became the estate's administra-

Masters had a successful law practice in Chicago. From 1903 to 1911 he was a partner of Clarence Darrow, best known for the Scopes Monkey Trial, in which he defended the right of a high school teacher to teach the theory of evolution.

tor, refused to honor the original agreement that she had signed. After a lengthy and complex trial and a series of appeals, Masters won, the original contract was upheld, and the disputed amount was put into trust for his client.

Family Life. Although Masters was a successful lawyer, he was a failure in his family life. On June 21, 1898, he married Helen Jenkins, and together they had three children: a son, Hardin, and two daughters, Marcia and Madeline. In both his own and his son's autobiographies, it is clear that Masters married Helen Jenkins not for love but because she was from a wealthy and influential family. Although Masters remained married to Helen for twenty-five years, he had numerous mistresses. The marriage ended in a messy divorce in 1923,

Masters married twice, neither time happily. Alienated from his first wife and three children, he lived with his second wife and their son in the Chelsea Hotel (seen in this photograph) in New York City.

and the three children never forgave their father for his treatment of their mother.

On November 5, 1926, Masters was married for a second time, to an English teacher named Ellen F. Coyne, with whom he had a son, Hilary. For almost twenty years the family lived in the Chelsea Hotel in New York's Greenwich Village. Frequently during their twenty-four years of marriage, however, Masters and his wife lived separately.

Literary Career. Even before he stopped practicing law in 1920, Edgar Lee Masters wrote extensively and considered himself a great American writer. Although he wrote fifty books, only *Spoon River Anthology* and *The New Spoon River* continue to interest readers. His biography of Abraham Lincoln, *Lincoln: The Man*, reveals little more than Masters's sympathy for the Confederacy. His biography *Walt Whitman* (1937) completely disregards

Whitman's homosexuality and fails to acknowledge the many different levels of meaning in his poetry. Masters's autobiography, *Across Spoon River*, reveals his egotism and insensitivity toward his two wives and four children, suggesting that if Edgar Lee Masters had written only his Spoon River poems, he might have left behind a more favorable and long-lasting legacy.

Final Years.
Masters's health declined throughout the 1940s. He published his last book, *The Sangamon*, in 1942, after which he became too ill to write. His wife Ellen committed him to Manhattan's Bellevue Hospital. Eventually, she transferred him to a nursing home in Melrose Park, Pennsylvania, close to the school at which she taught. Masters died in Melrose Park on March 5, 1950, and was buried three days later in Petersburg, Illinois.

HIGHLIGHTS IN MASTERS'S LIFE

1868   Edgar Lee Masters is born in Garnett, Kansas, on August 23.

1889   Graduates from Petersburg High School; enrolls at Knox College in Galesburg, Illinois.

1890   Begins law studies in his father's Petersburg, Illinois, law firm.

1891   Begins practicing law at his father's firm.

1892   Begins practicing law in Chicago.

1898   Marries Helen Jenkins; publishes his first volume of poetry, *A Book of Verses*.

1903–1911   Practices law with Clarence Darrow.

1915   Publishes his most famous book, *Spoon River Anthology*.

1917   Leaves his wife, Helen, and their three children.

1920   Stops practicing law; publishes novel, *Mitch Miller*, and book of poetry, *Domesday Book*.

1922   Publishes novel *Children of the Market Place*.

1923   Is divorced from wife, Helen.

1924   Publishes *The New Spoon River*.

1926   Marries Ellen Coyne, with whom he has a son, Hilary.

1931   Publishes the biography *Lincoln: The Man*.

1936   Publishes his autobiography, *Across Spoon River*

1937–1938   Publishes studies of Walt Whitman and Mark Twain.

1942   Publishes his last book, *The Sangamon*

1950   Dies on March 5, 1950, in Melrose Park, Pennsylvania; is buried in Petersburg, Illinois.

1970   Post Office Department issues a Masters commemorative stamp.

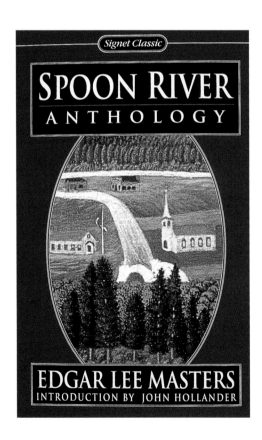

The Writer's Work

Edgar Lee Masters had two overlapping careers. From 1892 to 1920 he practiced law in Chicago, earning a reputation as an effective trial lawyer who represented the exploited poor. Despite his thriving legal career, he had lost interest in the law by the end of the 1910s, focusing more on his writing. Masters wrote plays, poetry, novels, biographies, an autobiography, and literary studies, but he is remembered mainly for two volumes of poetry: his masterpiece, *Spoon River Anthology*, and its sequel, *The New Spoon River*.

Masters's nonfiction works often reflect his personal opinions and prejudices. As a lifelong Democrat, Masters was openly antagonistic toward Republicans. His biography *Lincoln: The Man* surprised and displeased Illinois readers and historians alike with its harsh criticism of a universally admired local hero, Abraham Lincoln. Masters's dislike of

Of the fifty books Masters wrote during and after his law practice, only the two Spoon River anthologies were exceptional. His unfavorable biography of Abraham Lincoln, for instance, reveals little more than his own strong feelings for the Confederacy.

Ronald Primeau, in his book *Beyond Spoon River: The Legacy of Edgar Lee Masters* (1981), recognized that the poetry of Edgar Lee Masters did not have a definite influence on any later American poets. Instead, Primeau analyzed how Masters made creative use of such diverse sources as classical Greek poetry and the poetic works of Johann Wolfgang von Goethe, Ralph Waldo Emerson, Percy Bysshe Shelley, and Robert Browning. Masters's study of classical Greek epigrams taught him how to create poetry in which characters speak about their lives. From Goethe and Emerson, Masters learned how to give intellectual depth to his poetry using philosophical concepts.

In *Across Spoon River*, Masters describes the extraordinary effect of his year at Knox College in Galesburg, Illinois, from 1889 to 1890. Forty-six years after leaving Knox College, he still recalled discussing Johann Wolfgang von Goethe's *The Tragedy of Faust* (1808) with his German teacher, Professor Willard, and a fellow student of German descent. His reading of *Faust* and his Greek and Latin studies revealed to him the rich complexity of literature and philosophy and opened his mind to the intellectual life. Although he spent only one year at Knox College, he acknowledged the importance of this year on his later development as a writer. Significantly, after Masters's death, his elder son, Hardin, donated a collection of Master's books and manuscripts to Knox College.

A voracious reader, Masters especially loved romantic and ancient Greek poetry. Scholars attribute the intellectual depth of the Spoon River poems to his reading of, among others, the German poet Johann Wolfgang Goethe (1749–1832), pictured here.

President Lincoln was not only political, but also regional. Masters's family came from a southern state, Virginia, and he felt that the North should have allowed the South to secede from the Union. Masters also had a bias against African Americans, a sentiment that is apparent in his Lincoln biography. In his biography *Mark Twain: A Portrait* (1938), Masters attempts to psychoanalyze the famous writer, attributing to him unproven psychological problems.

Masters's critical comments about his parents and his first wife in his autobiography, *Across Spoon River*, enraged several family members, including his first wife and their two daughters. In this book, Masters refers to fifteen of his mistresses by their first names. He had mistresses during both of his marriages, and readers quickly conclude that Masters was indifferent to his wives' feelings and treated women as little more than sexual objects.

Major Themes in the Spoon River Poems. Masters spent his childhood and adolescence in the Sangamon Valley of central Illinois, northwest of Springfield. The

Spoon River flows through the small town of Lewistown, and railroads connected Lewistown to Petersburg, Springfield, and more distant cities. Despite the small-town setting of the Spoon River poems, readers identify with them, because each of the voices reveals a unique view of the human condition.

Scholars have determined that many characters in the Spoon River poems were inspired by actual people who lived in the nineteenth-century Sangamon Valley. However, readers do not need to know such facts to appreciate the complexity of the poems. The Spoon River poems deal with such issues as the conflicts between appearance and reality in small-town life, the conflicts among different social classes, the devastating effects of the Civil War, the loss of love, and personal tragedies of which others were often unaware.

Grant Wood's 1930 *Stone City* (Joslyn Art Museum, Omaha, Nebraska) calls to mind the small town of *Spoon River Anthology.* Many believe that Masters's fictional characters were inspired by local inhabitants of the Sangamon Valley of his childhood.

Spoon River Anthology opens and closes with multiple voices. A brief prologue entitled "The Hill" begins the collection and reveals that all the speakers are "sleeping on the hill," a fictional cemetery. The causes of death are diverse. Some were killed, others died during childbirth, others died in accidents, and still others from natural causes. The voices wonder where several of their friends are, but those who are buried do not know the fates of those who die after them. Solitude and separation — both during life and after death—are major themes in these two volumes.

The unnamed speakers in "The Hill" suggest that the lives of those buried in this cemetery have spanned a long period of American history. Some elderly residents spoke with soldiers who fought during the Revolutionary War; others saw and heard the local hero Abraham Lincoln. Some people died during the Civil War; still others lived and died during the fifty years between the end of the Civil War in 1865 and 1915, the year that *Spoon River Anthology* was published.

The haunting refrain of this poem is "All, all, are sleeping on the hill." The speakers in this book of poems desire to see clearly because they are now endowed with the pure understanding of beatific vision. The difficulty in seeing clearly is illustrated in the speech given by Dippold the Optician. The village optician encourages his listeners to try on different lenses so that they can see beyond the surface to deeper levels of reality. Each different lens permits the wearers to see people and things that now exist solely in their memories, but the final lens enables them to see pure light.

Other poems express the transformation of love from youthful passion into profound and mature love. The most exquisite love poem in his first Spoon River volume is the fourteen-line elegy spoken by a couple named William

POETRY

1898 A Book of Verses
1905 The Blood of the Prophets
1910 Songs and Sonnets
1912 Songs and Sonnets, Second Series
1915 Spoon River Anthology
1916 Songs and Satires
1916 The Great Valley
1918 Toward the Gulf
1919 Starved Rock
1920 Domesday Book
1921 The Open Sea
1924 The New Spoon River
1925 Selected Poems
1929 The Fate of the Jury: An Epilogue to Domesday Book
1930 Lichee Nuts
1933 The Serpent in the Wilderness
1935 Invisible Landscapes
1936 The Golden Fleece of California
1936 Poems of People
1937 The New World
1939 More People
1941 Illinois Poem
1942 Along the Illinois
1976 The Harmony of Deeper Music: Posthumous Poems

LONG FICTION

1920 Mitch Miller
1922 Children of the Market Place
1923 The Nuptial Flight
1923 Skeeters Kirby
1924 Mirage
1927 Kit O'Brien
1937 The Tide of Time

PLAYS

1907 Althea
1908 The Trifler
1909 The Leaves of the Tree
1910 Eileen
1910 The Locket
1911 The Bread of Idleness
1926 Lee: A Dramatic Poem

1928 Jack Kelso
1930 Gettysburg, Manila, Acoma
1931 Godbey
1934 Dramatic Duologues
1934 Richmond

NONFICTION

1927 Levy Mayer and the New Industrial Era
1931 Lincoln: The Man
1933 The Tale of Chicago
1935 Vachel Lindsay: A Poet in America
1936 Across Spoon River
1937 Walt Whitman
1938 Mark Twain: A Portrait
1942 The Sangamon

and Emily. They evoke the subtle links between life and death. Their lifelong love evolved from the "glow of youthful love" to "the sinking of the fire" before they finally "fade away together" in death. The poem ends with the lines, "That is a power of unison between souls / Like love itself!"

BIBLIOGRAPHY

Burgess, Charles E. "Spoon River: Politics and Poetry." *Papers on Language and Literature* 23, no. 3 (Summer 1987): 347–363.

Chandran, K. Narayana. "Revolt from the Grave: *Spoon River Anthology* by Edgar Lee Masters." *Midwest Quarterly* 29, no. 4 (Summer 1994): 438–447.

Flanagan, John T. *Edgar Lee Masters: The Spoon River Poet and His Critics*. Metuchen, N.J.: Scarecrow Press, 1974.

Hallwas, John E., ed. *The Vision of This Land: Studies on Vachel Lindsay, Edgar Lee Masters, and Carl Sandburg*. Macomb: Western Illinois University Press, 1976.

Hartley, Lois. *Spoon River Revisited*. Muncie, Ind.: Ball State University Press, 1963.

Masters, Hardin W. *Edgar Lee Masters: A Biographical Sketchbook About a Famous American Writer*. Cranbury, N.J.: Associate University Presses, 1978.

Primeau, Ronald. *Beyond Spoon River: The Legacy of Edgar Lee Masters*. Austin: University of Texas Press, 1981.

Russell, Herbert K. "Edgar Lee Masters." In *Dictionary of Literary Biography: American Poets, 1880–1945*, edited by Peter Quartermann. Detroit: Gale Research, 1981.

Wagner, Linda W. "Edgar Lee Masters: 1869–1950." In *American Writers: A Collection of Literary Biographies*, edited by Leonard Unger. New York: Charles Scribner's Sons, 1979.

Wrenn, John H. *Edgar Lee Masters*. Boston: Twayne Publishers, 1983.

Reader's Guide to Major Works

THE NEW SPOON RIVER

Genre: Poetry
Subgenre: Epitaphs
Published: New York, 1924
Time period: Early twentieth century
Setting: Fictional cemetery

Themes and Issues. Between 1915 and 1924, Edgar Lee Masters wrote numerous prose and verse works, but none enjoyed the popular and critical success of his *Spoon River Anthology*. Shortly before his divorce in 1923, he began writing *The New Spoon River*, which includes 324 epitaphs, but no prologue or epilogue. Early reviews were generally favorable, but the second Spoon River volume has not received as much scholarly attention as the first. It is unclear whether the epitaphs of *The New Spoon River* were based on specific Sangamon Valley residents, as were those of the previous volume. No annotated edition exists that places the epitaphs in a historical context.

The Poems. Some epitaphs were inspired by historical characters. In the epitaph spoken by Stephen Douglas, who debated Abraham Lincoln in the famous 1858 Illinois senate campaign, Senator Douglas explains that he won this election because he believed that only the "great race" (whites) and not the "small race" (African Americans) was entitled to full political liberty. He is proud that he supported

The river running through Robert Jordan's 1980 painting *Missouri Spring* brings to mind Masters's Spoon River. Like the first anthology, *The New Spoon River* featured the life stories of the dead but now included those of important historical characters as well.

the rights of the privileged, whereas his opponent Abraham Lincoln favored equality for "weak" (African American) people. Masters presents Stephen Douglas as an unrepentant racist.

Other epitaphs evoke the sufferings of everyday life by ordinary people in Spoon River. In his twelve-line epitaph, Claud Antle describes his unhappy life. He states in somewhat paranoid terms that, although some people are hunters, he was hunted. Other children mocked and physically attacked him during his youth. As a businessman he was "betrayed" and "robbed." Although he was a moral person who kept his dignity, he felt that he "was a deer compelled to live with the hounds." Claud Antle represents the image of an innocent but honest person whom immoral or amoral individuals seek to destroy.

Several poems in *The New Spoon River* make direct references to poems in the 1915 collection, and several themes are common to both volumes. In the original collection, Nellie speaks eloquently of the long-lasting trauma of rape. Similarly, Lucille Lusk in *The New Spoon River* talks about the exploitation and rape of women in the apparently calm village. She laments that Lucius Atherton "won" her virginity by raping her. She indicates that she was no different from many "spinsters of the church, patricians, grand ladies" who were also raped during their late childhood or adolescence.

Lucille's epitaph calls for a reexamination of Lucius Atherton's *Spoon River Anthology* epitaph. There, he describes himself as a "rural Don Juan." This comparison is entirely appropriate because, like the original Don Juan, he was a rapist. He reveled in his idea of himself as "an excellent knave of hearts" and regrets that in his later life, women no longer feared him.

As in the original collection, several epitaphs are spoken by those whom society has exploited. In his speech, Jerry Benson speaks out against the hypocrisy of self-righteous people who claim to favor morality but never raise their voices to protest the exploitation of the working class. Jerry was killed in an explosion caused by unsafe conditions at a local canning factory, but

not one commentator blamed the influential owners of the factory. Jerry states that this explosion killed not only him and his fellow workers but also their wives and children.

Analysis. Never able to re-create the success he enjoyed with *Spoon River Anthology*, Masters wrote *The New Spoon River* as a continuation of the first volume's style and theme. Masters continued to be inspired by real-life sources for the stories of his cemetery inhabitants, and many of his epitaphs build upon those in the previous volume, allowing a fuller, richer picture of life among the residents of Spoon River.

SOURCES FOR FURTHER STUDY

Flanagan, John T. *The Spoon River Poet*. Dallas, Tex.: Southern Methodist University Press, 1953.

Robinson, Frank K. *"The New Spoon River."* Austin: University of Texas Press, 1969.

Russell, Herbert. *Edgar Lee Masters' Literary Decline: From Spoon River to "The New Spoon River."* Carbondale: Southern Illinois University Press, 1980.

SPOON RIVER ANTHOLOGY

Genre: Poetry
Subgenre: Epitaphs
Published: New York, 1915
Time period: Early twentieth century
Setting: Fictional cemetery

Themes and Issues. With the additional poems added in 1916, the *Spoon River Anthology* comprises 247 epitaphs spoken by people buried in the Spoon River cemetery, a prologue entitled "The Hill," a poem called "The Spooniad," and an untitled epilogue. Each speaker gives his or her own view of life in Spoon River. Different characters often perceive certain family or village events from opposing perspectives.

The Poems. Two poems depict the loveless marriage of Ollie and Fletcher McGee. To all appearances, the McGees had a good marriage, but the reality was different. In the McGees' epitaphs, which Masters placed on facing pages, the two use almost the same terms to describe their unhappiness. Ollie describes how her husband "robbed" her of youth and beauty. Fletcher presents similar arguments, asserting that his wife somehow continues to "haunt" him after death. The two clearly despised each other, and each relied upon psychological manipulation to make the other miserable. Like Ollie McGee, Masters's first wife, Helen, felt unloved; when she asked Masters to discontinue his numerous affairs, he interpreted her requests as nagging. It is perhaps significant that the second and third epitaphs in this collection deal with a loveless marriage.

Not all of the poems in this collection express bitterness; some deal with unexpected and ironic events. In real life, Barney Hainsfeather was a Jewish merchant in Petersburg, where he experienced anti-Semitism daily. John Allen was a Presbyterian minister. Both Barney and John died in the same train accident. Because their bodies were so badly burned, an honest mistake was made: John was buried in a Jewish cemetery in Chicago and Barney was buried in a Christian cemetery in Petersburg. Barney ends his epitaph with the witty lament, "It was bad enough to run a clothing store in this town, / But to be buried here—*ach!*"

Numerous poems in this collection evoke the traumatic effects of the Civil War, both in central Illinois and throughout the nation. Since the first publication of *Spoon River Anthology* in 1915, American readers have admired the evocative force of its eloquent Civil War poems.

The cemetery of Andrew Wyeth's 1961 painting *Perpetual Care* could easily be that of Spoon River. Tales of regret, personal injustice, and overwhelming trauma all can be heard in Masters's epitaphs (tributes to the dead).

In the epitaph spoken by Knowlt Hoheimer, he tells of choosing between time in jail for stealing pigs and service in the Union army. He was killed at the beginning of the Battle of Missionary Ridge in 1863. When his body was brought back to Illinois, he was buried with full military honors, and the townsfolk had carved on his tombstone the Latin words "Pro Patria," a reference to the Latin saying "Quam dulce est pro patria mori," which translates, "How sweet it is to die for one's country." Knowlt does not know what these words mean.

Two of the most famous epitaphs in this collection, "Hannah Armstrong" and "Anne

Rutledge," deal with Abraham Lincoln, who lived and was buried in the nearby city of Springfield. The real Hannah Armstrong lived from 1810 to 1890 in the nearby town of New Salem. According to a local legend, Abraham Lincoln intervened personally so that her very ill son could be discharged from the Union army. Masters describes Hannah Armstrong as a poor and uneducated country woman who traveled to Washington, D.C., believing that the president himself would help her. When the guard would not let her into Lincoln's office, she yelled out, "Please say it's old Aunt Hannah Armstrong / From Illinois, come to see him about her sick boy / In the army." Lincoln stopped his business, spoke with her, and then personally wrote her son's discharge papers.

Another local legend was that Anne Rutledge, who died in 1835, was the woman Lincoln loved most; he left her to marry Mary Todd. "Anne Rutledge" has been probably been anthologized more frequently than any of Masters's poems. Although she was unknown during her short lifetime, she feels that her love for Lincoln gave meaning to her life because he would later make possible "the forgiveness of millions towards millions." In a wonderfully paradoxical statement, she tells her listeners that she was "Wedded to him, not through union, / But through separation."

Many poems deal with people who have been terribly mistreated by society. In her epitaph, Nellie Clark tells of being raped at the age of eight by a fifteen-year-old boy. The boy went unpunished for his crime, and Nellie's family did nothing to help her deal with her profound trauma. Two years after her marriage, her husband learned of the rape. When he left her because she had not been a virgin at her marriage, the villagers sided with him. Nellie was traumatized by the rapist, her husband, and the villagers, and she died shortly thereafter of a broken heart.

Shack Dye was an African American on whom white people in Spoon River played cruel jokes. They tormented and harassed him because of his race. Despite their public attempts to humiliate him, he kept his dignity, but they demonstrated their cruelty to others.

Other poems reflect the moral corruption of those whom society admired. John M. Church used his skill as an attorney for an insurance company so that juries and judges rejected all claims filed by widows and orphans whose husbands and fathers had been killed in a badly designed mine. The local bar association complimented him on his ingenious arguments. His insurance company and the mine owner escaped paying rightful claims, and the lives of the widows and orphans were destroyed. Now that he is dead, a rat has devoured his heart and a snake has made a nest in his skull. Justice has finally triumphed.

There is a spiritual dimension to several poems in the *Spoon River Anthology*. A beautiful epitaph spoken by a woman named Faith Matheny speaks of the brief glimpses of God humans are allowed during their lives. Since humans' understanding in this life is necessarily incomplete, they do not grasp, and their friends "may never tell," what these visions mean. Faith warns against the fear of death, because it will reveal "a splendor like the sun's." Through powerful images, she conveys the idea that incredible joy and peace may await in the next life. She ends her speech with beautiful lines to her listeners: "Be brave, all souls who have such visions! / As your body's alive as mine is dead, / You're catching a little whiff of the ether / Reserved for God Himself!"

Analysis. *Spoon River Anthology* is an extraordinary lyrical work with many different voices and styles. It includes social satire, wit, insights into the human condition, and meditations on the power of both human and divine love. Masters, in this collection, was among the first major twentieth-century American writer to emphasize the psychological aspects of the American character. Like the naturalists before him, he explored the social, political, biological, and sexual forces at work in a small town and how they impacted its inhabitants.

SOURCES FOR FURTHER STUDY

Murphy, Patrick D. "The Dialogical Voices of Edgar Lee Masters's *Spoon River Anthology*." *Studies in the Humanities* 15, no. 1 (June 1988): 13–22.

Narveson, Robert. "*Spoon River Anthology:* An Introduction." *Midamerica* 7 (1980): 52–72.

Timonedo, Emilio. "Meditations on *Spoon River Anthology:* The Epitaph as Life." *Quarterly Journal of Short Articles, Notes, and Reviews* 10 no. 3 (Summer 1997): 45–47.

Other Works

ACROSS SPOON RIVER (1936). Although Edgar Lee Masters wrote forty-eight works in addition to his two Spoon River collections of epitaphs, almost all his other works have fallen into oblivion. His autobiography, *Across Spoon River,* is, however, not without interest. In this book, he writes extensively of his friendship with two well-known writers, Theodore Dreiser and Carl Sandburg. His comments help us to better understand the early critical reception of their works, especially the poetry of Carl Sandburg, which later generations of readers held in much higher esteem than the poetry of Edgar Lee Masters.

In *Across Spoon River* Masters does not hesitate to criticize his parents, his first wife, and even President Woodrow Wilson, who chose not to appoint him as a federal judge, but he neither expresses the slightest remorse for any of his actions nor examines himself critically. His autobiography does, however, contain fascinating information about his formative years, his involvement in politics, and his legal career.

His autobiography reveals an extraordinary love for his grandparents and for the land in the Spoon River and Sangamon Valleys. Although he did not live in Lewistown or Petersburg during the last fifty-eight years of his life, his writings reveal his incredible love for this region of central Illinois.

THE TIDE OF TIME (1937). Although Edgar Lee Masters owes his literary fame almost exclusively to the beautifully crafted epitaphs in his two volumes of Spoon River poetry, his novels are also of value. Masters viewed his novels above all as vehicles in which to express his political and social beliefs. His fictional characters tend to be spokespersons for the novelist himself. This is clearly the case in his last novel, *The Tide of Time,* which was published in 1937.

Leonard Westerfield, the main character in this novel, is a thinly veiled imitation of the Democratic populist William Jennings Bryan, whom Edgar Lee Masters had supported in the

As depicted in Thomas Hart Benton's 1947 painting *Achelous and Hercules* (Smithsonian American Art Museum, Washington, D. C.), the transformation of America from an agrarian to industrial society was not a smooth transition. Masters saw it as a betrayal of the American heritage.

presidential election of 1896 against the winning candidate, William McKinley. Masters repeatedly bemoans the United States' betrayal of its agrarian roots by its election of candidates who pay more attention to urban concerns than to those of farmers.

Such nostalgia for rural America may have seemed rather artificial to Americans who were then struggling to survive during the Great Depression. Readers were unconcerned about the results of a presidential election that had taken place forty-one years earlier. As in his earlier novels, Masters treats a topic that was not of interest to his contemporary readers.

WALT WHITMAN (1937) Walt Whitman is generally recognized as one of America's greatest visionary poets. However, most early twentieth-century readers were familiar with few of his works, with the noticeable exception of his poem "O Captain, My Captain," written after the assassination of President Lincoln and frequently included in anthologies and literature textbooks. Masters's biography of Whitman was the first carefully researched biography of the poet.

Masters did not refer to Whitman's homosexuality, an avoidance which can be attributed either to society's homophobia or perhaps to Masters's own dislike for homosexuals. Masters notes that Whitman wrote no love poems to women and several to men, but he implies that Whitman was uninterested in love. Despite this shortcoming, Masters's book *Walt Whitman* gives a great deal of useful information about Whitman's creative and poetic evolution. Masters described in great detail the differences among the numerous editions of Whitman's masterpiece *Leaves of Grass*, which was first published in 1855 and revised several times until the publication in 1892 of the final edition. Masters suggested to scholars that they should examine the different versions of this acknowledged masterpiece of American poetry to fully appreciate Whitman's evolution as a poet.

Resources

The largest collection of manuscripts and books by Edgar Lee Masters was acquired by the University of Texas, Austin from his second son, Hilary, with the permission of Ellen Masters. Ellen Masters inherited manuscripts, books, letters, and photographs after her husband's death in 1950. These manuscripts inspired a good deal of research between the 1950s and the 1980s. Little of substance was published on Masters during the 1990s. However, the centenary of *Spoon River Anthology*'s original publication in the year 2015 may spark renewed interest in his works. Other sources of interest to students of Masters include the following:

Knox College Library, Galesburg, Illinois. Masters's first son, Hardin, contributed the books, letters, and manuscripts in his possession to the library of Knox College, which Masters attended from 1889 to 1890.

Spoon River Valley Scenic Drive. A scenic byway in Fulton County, Illinois, where Masters lived and set his *Spoon River Anthology*, winds through nearby towns, including Lewistown, where Masters's home still stands, and where the Oak Hill Cemetery, the inspiration for Masters's Spoon River poems, is located.

Video Recording. A play entitled *Spoon River Anthology*, which contains selected poems from the 1915 volume of epitaphs, was first staged and then recorded in 1965. A video recording of the play, part of the Master Poets Collection and entitled *Spoon River Anthology: A Poetic Portrait Gallery* (1997), is available.

Project Gutenberg. This online source of free electronic texts features the text of *Spoon River Anthology*. (http://www.sailor.gutenberg.org/etext98)

EDMUND J. CAMPION

Cormac McCarthy

BORN: July 20, 1933, Providence, Rhode Island
IDENTIFICATION: Late-twentieth-century novelist of the historic American South and West, known for his dark, apocalyptic narratives and soaring prose style.

Cormac McCarthy was first known for his nightmarish, fablelike novels set in the remote Appalachian wilderness of the American South. His unsettling books were praised by reviewers and critics but reached a relatively small audience. He earned a reputation as a "writer's writer" with his daring and distinctive style, which was sometimes compared with that of William Faulkner. A turning point in McCarthy's career came in 1985 with *Blood Meridian: Or, The Evening Redness in the West*, his first novel set in the historic American West. This violent book received little initial attention from reviewers but was later ranked with his best work. He gained national attention and phenomenal success with his next Western effort, *All the Pretty Horses* (1992). The book was a publishing sensation, and with the later volumes of his Border Trilogy, it secured both his popularity and his reputation as one of the major writers of his time.

Cormac McCarthy was born on July 20, 1933, in Providence, Rhode Island, to Charles Joseph McCarthy, an attorney, and his wife, Gladys Christina McGrail McCarthy. He was the eldest son and the third of six children: three boys and three girls. He was named Charles, after his father, and accounts differ as to whether his family or he himself later changed his name legally to Cormac, which is Gaelic for "son of Charles."

Childhood. In 1937 the family moved to Knoxville, Tennessee, where McCarthy's parents would live for the next thirty years. McCarthy's father took a job on the legal staff of the Tennessee Valley Authority (TVA), where he was promoted to the organization's chief counsel in 1958.

McCarthy was raised in the Roman Catholic faith, attending Knoxville's Catholic High School. After graduating in 1951, he enrolled at the University of Tennessee as a liberal arts major. In 1953 he left the university to join the air force and was stationed in Alaska, where he hosted a radio show.

College Years. After his military discharge in 1957, McCarthy returned to the University of Tennessee, where he published two short stories in the student literary magazine, *Phoenix*, under the byline C. J. McCarthy, Jr. He won the university's top creative-writing distinction, the Ingram-Merrill Award, in both 1959 and 1960. On January 3, 1961, he married Lee Holleman, a fellow student, and the couple had a son, Cullen.

McCarthy left the University of Tennessee without a degree and moved with his family to Chicago, where he worked for a period of time as an auto mechanic while writing his first novel, eventually published as *The Orchard Keeper* (1965). The McCarthys moved to Sevier County, Tennessee, where the couple subsequently divorced.

Early Success. McCarthy's writing, though still unpublished, earned him a travel fellowship from the American Academy of Arts and Letters in 1965. McCarthy took an ocean cruise to the British Isles, intending to visit the homeland

The barren scene outside the Clarence Brown Theater of Performing Arts at the University of Tennessee is in stark contrast with the growth McCarthy experienced at the university. His writing career began to bud during his time at the University of Tennessee, where he was bestowed the school's top creative writing award two years in a row.

Ibiza, the third largest of the Balearic Islands, situated in the western Mediterranean Sea, fostered creativity in artists and writers alike. It was more than likely a combination of the history, people, and natural beauty that drew artists to the area in the 1960s. McCarthy was among them.

of his Irish ancestors. Later that year, *The Orchard Keeper* was published by Random House in New York, where McCarthy's first editor was Albert Erskine, who had a long professional relationship with the southern writer William Faulkner. Although its sales were modest, McCarthy's first novel received largely favorable reviews.

During his Atlantic cruise, McCarthy met Anne DeLisle, a British performer who was working aboard the ship, and the two were married in England in 1966. That year McCarthy received a grant from the Rockefeller Foundation, which allowed him and his wife to tour England, France, Italy, and Spain while McCarthy worked on his second novel, *Outer Dark* (1968). The couple eventually chose to live on Ibiza, a Mediterranean island with a growing reputation as an artists' colony.

In 1967 the McCarthys moved to Rockford, Tennessee, where they rented a small farmhouse. *Outer Dark* was published the following year to good reviews but modest sales. In 1969 McCarthy received a Guggenheim Fellowship, and he and his wife renovated and moved into an old barn near Louisville, Tennessee.

In the meantime McCarthy worked on his third novel, *Child of God* (1973), which is loosely based on actual historic events in Sevier County. *Child of God* was published to mixed reviews, some of them condemning McCarthy's choice of dark subjects, including necrophilia. His next project, also historically based, was a screenplay for a PBS film production, *The Gardener's Son*, telecast in January, 1977. By then, he and Anne DeLisle had separated, with no children. McCarthy moved to El Paso, Texas, and the couple later divorced.

Throughout most of McCarthy's adulthood, his shunning of traditional publicity, combined with his nomadic and intensely private lifestyle, resulted in a scarcity of biographical information—leading one literary columnist to refer to him as "the greatest writer you've never heard of."

Wider Recognition. In 1979 McCarthy published his fourth and most ambitious novel to that time. He had written and polished *Suttree*—a dark tragicomedy set in 1950s Memphis—periodically from the beginning of his writing career. Many reviewers recognized it as his best work to date, and it was instrumental in McCarthy's being awarded his most prestigious grant yet, a MacArthur Fellowship in 1981.

Western Focus. McCarthy used the MacArthur grant money to write and travel in Texas and Mexico, researching historical events of the 1840s as the basis for a surreal, apocalyptic Western that would be published in 1985 as *Blood Meridian*. The violent and disturbing novel received surprisingly little attention from reviewers at the time, with some critics suggesting that he should return to his southern settings. In retrospect, however, *Blood Meridian* marked a major turning point in McCarthy's writing—all of his subsequent novels have been Westerns—and a number of critics still consider *Blood Meridian* his greatest literary achievement.

When McCarthy's longtime Random House editor, Albert Erskine, retired, McCarthy moved to the publishing house of Alfred A. Knopf. There, the young, high-profile editor Gary Fisketjon convinced McCarthy to give his first substantial interview with a reporter for the *New York Times Magazine*, to coincide with the 1992 publication of his novel *All the Pretty Horses*. The book not only received high praise from reviewers but also became McCarthy's first best-seller, selling over 190,000 hardcover copies in six months. McCarthy reportedly celebrated his success by buying a new pickup

Penelope Cruz and Matt Damon starred in the 2000 film adaptation of McCarthy's coming-of-age novel *All the Pretty Horses*, eight years after the publication of the book. The experience proved to be a coming-of-age for McCarthy as well: It was his first best-seller.

truck and digging in to write the next two novels of what he called his Border Trilogy.

In 1994 McCarthy edited and published *The Stonemason*, a play he had written in the 1970s. That same year, Knopf published the second novel in his Border Trilogy, *The Crossing*. Its sales outdistanced even those of *All the Pretty Horses*; an unusually large first printing of 200,000 copies sold so rapidly that a second printing was required in less than a month.

The third Border Trilogy volume, *Cities of the Plain*, was published in 1998. There is evidence that much of its material was written in screenplay form long before the other two volumes of the trilogy were begun. That same year, McCarthy was married for a third time, to Jennifer Winkley, a graduate of the University of Texas at El Paso.

HIGHLIGHTS IN McCARTHY'S LIFE

1933 Cormac McCarthy is born Charles McCarthy, Jr., on July 20 in Providence, Rhode Island.

1937 Moves with family to Knoxville, Tennessee.

1951 Graduates from Catholic High School; enrolls at University of Tennessee.

1953 Joins the air force and is stationed in Alaska.

1957 Returns to the University of Tennessee; publishes his first short stories in campus magazine.

1959 Wins the university's Ingram-Merrill Award and wins another the following year.

1961 Marries Lee Holleman; their son, Cullen is born; the couple later divorce.

1965 McCarthy publishes his first novel, *The Orchard Keeper*; receives American Academy of Arts and Letters fellowship; travels to the British Isles and Western Europe.

1966 Marries Anne DeLisle in Great Britain.

1967 Returns to America; settles with second wife in Rockford, Tennessee.

1968 Publishes *Outer Dark*.

1969 Receives Guggenheim Fellowship; moves to Louisville, Tennessee.

1973 Publishes *Child of God*.

1977 His teleplay *The Gardener's Son* is broadcast on PBS; McCarthy is divorced from second wife; moves to El Paso, Texas.

1979 Publishes *Suttree*.

1981 Receives MacArthur Fellowship.

1985 Publishes *Blood Meridian*.

1992 Publishes his first best-seller, *All the Pretty Horses*.

1994 Edits and publishes play *The Stonemason*; publishes *The Crossing*.

1998 Is married for the third time, to Jennifer Winkley; publishes *Cities of the Plain*.

1999 Screen version of *All the Pretty Horses* is filmed.

Actor Henry Thomas, who plays the role of Rawlins, on the set of *All the Pretty Horses*

The Writer's Work

Cormac McCarthy's writing career can be divided into two distinct periods: from 1965 to 1979, his "southern" years, during which he published four novels set in the Appalachian region of America, and after 1979, since which time he has published four novels set in the American West.

Common Characteristics in McCarthy's Fiction. Although it varies greatly in setting and theme, McCarthy's writing has many common characteristics. One is a richly beautiful and magisterial prose style that frequently contrasts with the bleakness and ugliness of human behavior and events described in the narrative. One critic referred to McCarthy—not pejoratively—as "word-drunk."

Other characteristics of McCarthy's work include an obsession with dark, sometimes evil and depraved, characters from the underside of society; a depiction of characters with dialogue and action rather than with internal thoughts and observations; a theologically intense concentration on death, fate, human evil, and the relationship of humankind to God; a tendency to subvert popular societal myths such as the basic goodness of simple rural people and the glorious conquering of America's West; and a flawless ear for the infinite subtleties of regional dialect in conversation. McCarthy also often renders sections of spoken Spanish without translation for the reader.

The leading McCarthy scholar, Edwin T. Arnold, notes that although McCarthy's work

A lone figure leads his horse across the New Mexican landscape. McCarthy's western novels are filled with independent spirits. Some reviewers see these solitary cowboys as clichés, but in the hands of McCarthy, the men emerge as complex, multifaceted characters.

Spirituality and mysterious notions of God loom large in the work of McCarthy. Often his protagonists struggle to rectify their isolation in the world with the idea of a higher existence.

contains such dark, gothic elements as "incest, infanticide, necrophilia; drunkenness, debauchery, sacrilege; physical deformity and spiritual morbidity," to focus mainly on these sensational aspects of his fiction would be to miss the "essential religiosity" at its core.

Religious Themes. This examination of religious ideas is often presented as monologues or debates between characters, some of whom are ex-priests. The title character of *Suttree* is a lapsed Catholic who nonetheless is haunted by the church, the notion of death, and the memory of his stillborn twin brother. At one point, Suttree observes, "If our dead kin are sainted we may rightly pray to them. Mother Church tells us so . . . I followed him into the world, me. . . . And used to pray for his soul days past."

McCarthy's fictional representation of God is most often as a wild and often brutal figure who is mostly unknowable but whose presence continually beckons. Perhaps the best example of this paradoxical beckoning comes in *The Crossing*, when an ex-priest tells the protagonist Billy Parham that "men do not turn from God so easily you see. Not so easily. Deep in each man is the knowledge that something knows of his existence. Something knows, and cannot be fled nor hid from. To imagine otherwise is to imagine the unspeakable. . . ."

Themes of Nature. Another of McCarthy's preoccupations is the conundrum of the individual's relationship to the landscape and to fellow creatures. The author's long, idyllic descriptions of mountains, sunsets, rivers,

SOME INSPIRATIONS BEHIND McCARTHY'S WORK

Cormac McCarthy's Catholic upbringing influenced both his worldview and his writing, a perspective nascent in his earlier work but far more pronounced in *Suttree*, *Blood Meridian*, and the Border Trilogy.

In *Blood Meridian* and the novels of the Border Trilogy, these "mocking intimations of grace" take on ever more dark and changing guises, including that which a number of critics identify as a hint of gnosticism, an esoteric religious movement that challenged second- and third-century orthodox Christianity. According to gnostic thought, the material universe is wholly evil and populated by sparks of the Divine Being, that have fallen from the transcendent realm and are imprisoned in the bodies of human beings. Gnostic belief holds that only knowledge, or gnosis, can reawaken the divine element in humanity and release it from its bondage to the material world.

Another important influence on McCarthy's fiction is the tradition of oral storytelling central to southern writing. His characters are continually listening to and telling stories. Some of the stories bear on the situation at hand, while others seem rendered solely for the purpose of the telling. Characters are sometimes met at remote places by a stranger whose only function is to tell them a story before receding into the periphery. In *All the Pretty Horses*, a young boy is warned by an older character, "Evil is a true thing. It goes about on its own legs. Maybe some day it will come to visit you. Maybe it already has."

horses, wolves, and hawks are hauntingly and unsentimentally poetic. In what is by far the most violent and challenging of McCarthy's novels, *Blood Meridian*, a Mexican bandit remarks to a boy, "When the lambs is lost in the mountain . . . they is cry. Sometimes come the mother. Sometimes the wolf."

BIBLIOGRAPHY

Amiran, Eyal. "Riding Against the Plot." *American Book Review* 14 (February/March 1993): 16, 23.

Arnold, Edwin T. "Blood and Grace: The Fiction of Cormac McCarthy." *Commonweal* 121 (November 4, 1994): 11–16.

Arnold, Edwin T., and Dianne C. Luce, eds. *Perspectives on Cormac McCarthy*. Jackson: University of Mississippi Press, 1999.

Bell, Vereen M. *The Achievement of Cormac McCarthy*. Baton Rouge: Louisiana State University Press, 1988.

Cawelti, John G. "Cormac McCarthy: Restless Seekers." In *Southern Writers at Century's End*, edited by Jeffrey J. Folks and James A. Perkins. Lexington: University Press of Kentucky, 1997.

Ditsky, John. "Further into Darkness: The Novels of Cormac McCarthy." *Hollins Critic* 18 (April 1981).

Hall, Wade, and Rich Wallach. *Sacred Violence: A Reader's Companion to Cormac McCarthy*. El Paso: Texas Western Press, 1995.

Jarrett, Robert L. *Cormac McCarthy*. New York: Twayne Publishers, 1997.

Williams, Don. "All the Pretty Colors of Cormac McCarthy (Has the Master of the Macabre Gone Soft?)." *Chattahoochee Review* 13, no. 4 (Summer 1993).

Winchell, Mark Royden. "Inner Dark: Or, The Place of Cormac McCarthy." *Southern Review* 26 (April 1990).

Reader's Guide to Major Works

ALL THE PRETTY HORSES
Genre: Novel
Subgenre: Historical fiction
Published: New York, 1992
Time period: 1949
Setting: Texas; Mexico

Themes and Issues. When Cormac McCarthy's much anticipated and relatively slim novel *All the Pretty Horses* appeared, the initial response was one of puzzlement. The quality of McCarthy's writing was not in question; the novel won that year's National Book Award and National Book Critics Circle Award for fiction. However, the subject matter and approach of *All the Pretty Horses*—particularly in contrast to those of its apocalyptic predecessor, *Blood Meridian*—seemed to signal a radical change of direction for McCarthy. The lyrical coming-of-age story was far more in the realm of a conventional Western, with a somewhat restrained prose style and universal themes of love, courage, and loyalty.

The Plot. In the years after World War II, sixteen-year-old John Grady Cole lives on a small Texas ranch with his grandfather, with whom he has lived since his parents' separation. He finds himself rootless in the world when his grandfather dies and leaves the failing ranch to John Grady's mother, who plans to sell it. Cole and his good friend Rawlins decide to go on a horseback quest to Mexico. Along the way the boys meet an impulsive young wanderer named Jimmy Blevins. Against their better judgment, they allow Blevins to join them.

Once across the border, they find a totally different and sinister world—and far more adventure—than they had imagined. After Blevins is pursued by armed men, Cole and Rawlins flee a small town and come across the palatial ranch of an aristocrat, Don Hector. They take a job breaking the wild mountain horses that the rancher breeds with his own stock. Against others' advice, Cole falls in love with Alejandra, the don's rebellious young daughter. Before long, both Cole and Rawlins find themselves arrested and put in the same jail with Blevins, who has been charged with murder and is later executed. Prison life is violent, and Cole finds himself killing a man in self-defense. The two boys are mysteriously released from prison, and Cole naïvely goes in search of Alejandra, only to find that she chooses her family's power and money over his love.

Devastated, Cole returns home and finds his father and his childhood nurse both dead. He is older and wiser, but his victory is a mixed one. The poignant ending clearly invites a sequel.

Santiago Perez's oil painting *Drifter* is emblematic of many of McCarthy's characters, adventuresome and often headstrong young loners who are never sure what lies ahead.

Analysis. This first novel in McCarthy's Border Trilogy further established his status as a major American writer. It marked a shift in his work from his earlier gothic excesses to a more lyrical and nostalgic examination of the American Southwest. The publication of the remaining two Border Trilogy volumes, *The Crossing* and *Cities of the Plain*—neither of which are sequels in the traditional sense—has demanded a complex critical reassessment of all three works, both individually and in the context of the resounding echoes from retold tales.

SOURCES FOR FURTHER STUDY

Amiran, Eyal. "Riding Against the Plot." *American Book Review* 14 (February/March 1993): 16, 23.

Luce, Dianne C. "The Road and the Matrix: The World as Tale in *The Crossing*." In *Perspectives on Cormac McCarthy*, edited by Edwin T. Arnold and Dianne C. Luce. Jackson: University of Mississippi Press, 1999.

Morrison, Gail Moore. "*All the Pretty Horses*: John Grady Cole's Expulsion from Paradise." In *Perspectives on Cormac McCarthy*, edited by Edwin T. Arnold and Dianne C. Luce. Jackson: University of Mississippi Press, 1999.

BLOOD MERIDIAN: OR, THE EVENING REDNESS IN THE WEST

Genre: Novel
Subgenre: Historical fiction
Published: New York, 1985
Time period: Late 1840s
Setting: Texas-Mexico borderlands

Themes and Issues. Critics have variously suggested that McCarthy's almost unthinkably violent epic *Blood Meridian* is either his most troubling or his greatest book—and sometimes both at once—as it subverts the mythology of America's westward expansion and lays bare its underside of violence and depravity.

The narrative is firmly based in documented historical events, centering on roving gangs of scalp-hunting outlaws contracted by territorial governors in the 1840s to clear the borderlands of American Indians. McCarthy, though, takes the historical facts to a bizarre and horrifying level of realism—or surrealism—that has led some critics to compare the novel with the classic writings of Dante Alighieri and the Marquis de Sade, to the violent action films of the late-twentieth-century director Sam Peckinpah, and to the death-obsessed works of the early-sixteenth-century painter Hieronymus Bosch.

The Plot. A fourteen-year-old Tennessee boy, a runaway identified only as the Kid, drifts aimlessly on riverboats until he ends up in Nacogdoches, Texas. At a tent revival meeting, he encounters a huge, pale, monstrous, funny genius of a rogue, whom he later comes to know as Judge Holden, and he hires on with a group of soldiers setting off to make their fortune in neighboring Mexico.

In the bleak, morally bereft landscape of the borderlands, the Kid gradually discovers that there are no good or bad causes, only the unending savagery of both the Native Americans and their would-be conquerors. At the center of the action is the Judge, who controls his gang of soldiers through fear, wit, and his innate mastery of human nature. The Judge is a fanatically accomplished naturalist and a talented fiddler and dancer. He has a massive intellect and can discourse at length on science, history, and languages. He is also, as the Kid discovers, a sadistic killer and child molester. At one point, the Judge states his basic philosophy: "If war is not holy, man is nothing but antic clay."

Camaraderie and the need for companionship on the vast, lonely stretches of the range are central to McCarthy's western novels. His work can be viewed as intricate studies of men, their close friendships and their explosive violence, as well.

The bloodbath escalates beyond all seeming limits, and the soldiers suffer disastrous casualties. Eventually only the Judge and the Kid remain standing to play out the battle for survival.

Analysis. The horror and ambitious scope of *Blood Meridian* seem—willfully, at times—to defy rational analysis as it explores themes of regeneration through violence. Critics have called this novel McCarthy's masterpiece, comparing it with the works of Herman Melville and William Faulkner.

SOURCES FOR FURTHER STUDY

Daugherty, Leo. "Gravers False and True: *Blood Meridian* as Gnostic Tragedy." In *Perspectives on Cormac McCarthy*, edited by Edwin T. Arnold and Dianne C. Luce. Jackson: University of Mississippi Press, 1999.

Sepich, John Emil. "'What kind of indians was them?': Some Historical Sources in Cormac McCarthy's *Blood Meridian*." In *Perspectives on Cormac McCarthy*, edited by Edwin T. Arnold and Dianne C. Luce. Jackson: University of Mississippi Press, 1999.

Shaviro, Steven. "The Very Life of the Darkness: A Reading of *Blood Meridian*." In *Perspectives on Cormac McCarthy*, edited by Edwin T. Arnold and Dianne C. Luce. Jackson: University of Mississippi Press, 1999.

SUTTREE

Genre: Novel
Subgenre: Picaresque tragicomedy
Published: New York, 1979
Time period: 1951
Setting: Knoxville, Tennessee

Themes and Issues. Despite its obvious Deep South setting on and around the Tennessee River as well as its powerful evocation of both pastoral and urban landscapes, *Suttree* bears a strong kinship with James Joyce's *Ulysses* (1922). It is not difficult to envision McCarthy's river wanderer, Cornelius Suttree, as a modern successor to Joyce's Leopold Bloom. Although *Suttree* is generally considered the most humorous of McCarthy's novels, the humor has a dark edge. Suttree's search for peace, enlightenment, and good fishing is repeatedly foiled by a motley cast of characters in whose lives he becomes, for better or worse, entangled: drunks, thieves, transvestites, con artists, preachers, prostitutes, grave diggers, blind hermits, a dwarf witch, and others.

The Plot. Cornelius Suttree, with a college education and a privileged background, has abandoned his family, wife, and young son to live alone on a houseboat moored beneath a bridge on the Tennessee River. From this modest headquarters, he wanders the slums of Knoxville, Tennessee. The slums lure him both literally and figuratively from the river to which he has in a sense apprenticed himself to learn its "indefatigable will" in the face of all human assaults and interventions—including, in the novel's opening scene, a suicide who leaps from the bridge above Suttree's houseboat.

In *Suttree*, the title character shirks responsibility and the conventions of a traditional life for the solitude of a houseboat. The houseboat becomes a symbol of fluidity and isolation, but Cornelius Suttree cannot shut out the world forever. It arrives in the form of a new highway.

To say that *Suttree* is not conventionally plotted is an understatement. Many of the novel's most poignant and hilarious episodes occur around Gene Harrogate, a young man whom Suttree meets first in a prison workhouse and again after their release and who styles himself as Suttree's sidekick. Harrogate is one of the most original and memorable comic characters in modern fiction. He is not easy for Suttree to protect and still less so to like, but Suttree's paternal instincts—likely driven in part by the death of his own son—are faithful and long-suffering. Harrogate's misadventures range from his sexually molesting a farmer's watermelons to his stealing dynamite in order to blow up a cave and get rich by mining and selling the cave's immense stores of bat manure.

At the novel's end—with his isolated river retreat threatened by a new highway system and his life threatened by typhoid fever—Suttree has a delirious dream of confessing before a priest that he has squandered his life. In a final grace note, Suttree recovers from his illness, is given a ladle of cool water by an angelic-looking child, and is offered a free ride to another town.

Analysis. Owing to its density, odd tone, and offbeat complexity, *Suttree* has met with a variety of critical interpretations. Some contend that the work is existential and "ambiguously nihilistic," its characters "almost without thoughts," and its symbols confusing and ultimately without meaning. Others take the almost opposite view that *Suttree* is perhaps McCarthy's most religious book, deeply involved with questions of theology and morality.

McCarthy's characters are driven by the universal emotions of love, loneliness, guilt, shame, hope, and despair. His stories all focus on these issues, and in each there is a measure by which the characters' failure or success may be judged. Although McCarthy's work is known for its violence, mystery, and chaos, it also displays an inherently religious conviction. Even in McCarthy's darkest stories, there is opportunity for redemption through grace.

SOURCES FOR FURTHER STUDY

Longley, John Lewis, Jr. "*Suttree* and the Metaphysics of Death." *Southern Literary Journal* 17 (1985): 79–90.

Shelton, Frank W. "*Suttree* and Suicide." *Southern Quarterly* 29, no. 1 (1990): 71–83.

Spencer, William C. "Altered States of Consciousness in *Suttree*." *Southern Quarterly* 35, no. 2 (Winter 1997): 87–92.

Young, Thomas D., Jr. "The Imprisonment of Sensibility: *Suttree*." In *Perspectives on Cormac McCarthy*, edited by Edwin T. Arnold and Dianne C. Luce. Jackson: University of Mississippi Press, 1999.

Other Works

CHILD OF GOD (1973). The most challenging and controversial of Cormac McCarthy's early novels, *Child of God* has as its title character an outcast named Lester Ballard, who ends up living in underground caves with the prizes of his depraved lifestyle: giant stuffed animals he has won at carnivals and the decaying bodies of men and women he has shot to death.

The novel opens with the auctioning of Ballard's family's farm. Ballard moves to an abandoned cabin and begins prowling garbage dumps and quarries, looking for cast-off items that strike his fancy. Another of his favorite haunts is the local lover's lane, where he becomes aroused by spying on couples parked in their darkened cars. There he meets a deserted prostitute, and his sincere attempt to reach out to her is repaid with her false accusation of rape.

This scene is the catalyst for Ballard's resultant killing spree and his ever-deepening descent into madness and necrophilia. He forms a plan to kill the man who bought his farm, while a sheriff, aptly named Fate Turner, tries to solve Ballard's serial murders. The irony and triumph of *Child of God* is the tender and reconciliatory tone with which McCarthy recounts even Ballard's most vile deeds, at one point directly comparing the protagonist to the reader: "A child of God much like yourself perhaps."

Finally captured, Ballard dies in an asylum. The novel ends with a scene at a morgue in which medical students dissect his body for their studies.

THE ORCHARD KEEPER (1965). McCarthy's first published novel, set in the small Tennessee town of Red Branch, is the story of three main characters: John Wesley Rattner, a young boy whose father has been murdered; Rattner's uncle Ather Ownby, a fiercely independent hermit and woodsman; and a local bootlegger, Marion Sylder. John Wesley considers Sylder his hero, unaware that the bootlegger is his father's killer and that his father's corpse has lain for years in a pit next to Ownby's apple orchard. Ownby conscientiously guards the corpse, unaware of its identity.

The relationship between the three is threatened, as civilization, in the form of, among other things, a bullying deputy sheriff named Legwater, closes in on their idyllic and remote mountain existence. The author's rendering of the mountains, forests, and streams is so pervasive and lyrical that some critics have noted that the natural world is another of the novel's characters. Red Branch is, however, no edenic garden. The setting of *The Orchard Keeper* can be as unforgiving as the bleak desert landscapes in McCarthy's later writing and as violent as the characters themselves.

OUTER DARK (1968). Somewhat similar in tone and setting to *The Orchard Keeper*, this novel is nevertheless different in approach. The story seems to take place outside normal constraints of time and logic, as though occurring in a fable or a dream—or more appropriately, a nightmare.

Culla Home and his sister, Rinthy, live alone in the remote mountains, and their incestuous relationship has produced a baby whom, near the book's beginning, Culla takes into the woods and leaves to die. Rinthy doubts the story he tells and goes looking for the baby's shallow grave, which she finds empty.

Rinthy goes in search of her lost child, convinced that the child is with an itinerant tinkerer who recently visited their cabin. Culla wanders the landscape as well, supposedly in search of his sister, although his actions reveal this is not a priority.

True to the parable-like quality of the tale, the gentle and innocent Rinthy tends to make serendipitous contacts with those she meets, while her brother's are less exciting. Continually threatening are three shadowy, monstrous figures—rumored to be grave robbers, cannibals, and worse—who also roam the wilderness. The reader knows that Culla and Rinthy must eventually cross paths with this threatening trio.

Ross Dickinson's 1934 oil painting *Valley Farms* (Smithsonian American Art Museum, Washington, D.C.) captures the spirit of people struggling against and triumphing over the land. The forbidding landscapes that color McCarthy's novels become extensions of the minds of his protagonists, boundless and uncharted.

Resources

Much information about Cormac McCarthy exists on line. Some sources of interest to students of McCarthy include the following:

Cormac McCarthy Society. The society is the most comprehensive on-line source for information on McCarthy's work and the growing body of critical literature about his life and writing. The society also conducts annual conferences and mini-conferences and publishes a twice-annual newsletter. (http://www.cormacmccarthy.com)

The Cormac McCarthy Journal. This peer-reviewed journal is published in both print and on-line versions and features articles providing historical background and critical analysis of McCarthy's works. (http://www.cormacmccarthy.com/journal/)

Southwestern Literature Home Page. This site, run by a professor at New Mexico State University, offers a biography of McCarthy with cited sources. Also featured are student comments on McCarthy that may be helpful to other students and links to sites relevant to *The Crossing*. (http://web.nmsu.edu/~tomlynch/swlit.mccarthy.html)

CARROLL DALE SHORT

Carson McCullers

BORN: February 19, 1917, Columbus, Georgia
DIED: September 29, 1967, Nyack, New York
IDENTIFICATION: Mid-twentieth-century southern writer noted for her portraits of spiritually isolated individuals in novels, short stories, and plays.

Carson McCullers published her first novel, *The Heart Is a Lonely Hunter* (1940), at the age of twenty-three and was acclaimed a literary wunderkind. She was a contemporary of Tennessee Williams, Flannery O'Connor, Eudora Welty, Katherine Anne Porter, and other southern writers whose simple often grotesque characters explore the fundamental sadness of the human condition. Her most highly regarded fiction, published in the 1940s, deals with loneliness and alienation in ways that transcend her mostly southern settings.

The Writer's Life

Carson McCullers was born Lula Carson Smith on February 19, 1917, in Columbus, Georgia. She was the oldest of three children born to Lamar Smith, a jeweler from Alabama, and Marguerite Waters Smith. McCullers was named for her maternal grandmother, a descendant of an Irish family that settled in South Carolina before the American Revolution, with whom the family lived.

Childhood. McCullers enjoyed a comfortable middle-class upbringing in Columbus, a mill town located across the Chattahoochee River from Alabama. There she absorbed the town's local color and observed many of the personalities and character types that would later figure in her tales of the South. She and her siblings were raised as Baptists. She enjoyed a close relationship with her family, especially her mother, who believed McCullers to be precocious and destined for greatness.

In 1926 McCullers began taking piano lessons and showed such proficiency that it was assumed she would embark on a career as a concert pianist. In 1930 she began studying with Mary Tucker, a piano teacher whose husband was stationed at the nearby U.S. Army base, Fort Benning, Georgia. That year, McCullers dropped her given first name and began calling herself Carson. She flourished under Tucker's instruction and bonded with Tucker and her family. When the Tuckers moved in 1934, McCullers abandoned her musical ambitions.

The Young Writer. McCullers was a bookish child. She was considered eccentric and quirky, and she was taller than most of her classmates. Although only an average student, she began writing shortly after beginning music lessons. By the time she was a teenager, she was familiar with the plays of Eugene O'Neill and the fiction of the Russian writers Fyodor Dostoevski and Anton Chekhov. At fifteen, she suffered a bout of rheumatic fever, the first of many serious illnesses. During her convalescence she wrote an unpublished novel and decided that she was inclined more toward writing than music.

With money made by selling a diamond ring from her grandmother, McCullers moved to New York in

Carson McCullers was born Lula Carson Smith in Columbus, Georgia, the mill town shown in this 1913 photograph. It is the people of this town who would later help shape the characters in her stories.

1934, ostensibly to study piano at Juilliard. However, she never enrolled there and instead took creative writing classes with Sylvia Chatfield Bates at New York University and Whit Burnett at Columbia University, supporting herself at odd jobs. In 1936 Burnett selected her story "Wunderkind" for publication in *Story* magazine.

Marriage and Early Success.

McCullers spent the summer of 1935 at home in Georgia, where she met Reeves McCullers, a young soldier from Alabama stationed at nearby Fort Benning who also nursed dreams of writing. With the encouragement of her family, who thought Reeves's outgoing personality a good counterbalance to her introspective nature, she and Reeves married

Married in 1937, divorced in 1942, and remarried in 1945, Carson and Reeves McCullers had a tormented relationship that was marred by his alcoholism and her poor health. Reeves eventually committed suicide in 1953.

in the fall of 1937. The couple moved to Fayetteville, North Carolina, where Reeves took a job as a credit investigator.

During her honeymoon, McCullers began a novel she entitled, "The Mute." Six chapters and an outline of the novel won her second place and a $500 advance in a contest for new writers sponsored by Houghton Mifflin. McCullers completed the manuscript in 1939, and it was published in 1940 as *The Heart Is a Lonely Hunter*. Reviews were unanimously favorable, declaring the twenty-three-year-old McCullers a literary prodigy.

Personal Problems.

By the time of the novel's publication, the McCullerses' marriage was disintegrating. She had moved with Reeves to New York shortly before the publication of *The Heart Is a Lonely Hunter*. Her second novel, published in 1941 as *Reflections in a Golden Eye*, is thought to chronicle the growing tensions between her and her husband. Written in a span of two months, the novel is dedicated to the Swiss writer Annemarie Clarac-Schwarzenbach, whom McCullers took as her lover shortly after moving to New York. Reeves had also begun a homosexual relationship.

In the fall of 1940, McCullers returned from a fellowship at the Bread Loaf Writers' Conference at Middlebury College in Vermont and moved from the apartment she shared with Reeves to Brooklyn. There she joined a literary circle that included Paul Bowles, Richard Wright, and W. H. Auden. The following February, she suffered a disabling stroke. By the summer, she was able to attend a writer's retreat at Yaddo in Saratoga Springs, New York, the first of many visits she would make there. She began writing *The Member of the Wedding* (1946) but postponed its completion to work on her well-known novella, *The Ballad of the Sad Café* (1951).

McCullers divorced Reeves in 1942, and Reeves reenlisted in the army the same year, taking a commission as company commander in the U.S. Rangers. The same year, McCullers

The author is seen here with Harold Clurman, who in 1950 directed the Broadway stage adaptation of *The Member of the Wedding* (1946), her best-known story and the last of her most important works. It won the New York Drama Critics Circle Award for best play.

Stage Success.

Under the direction of Harold Clurman, *The Member of the Wedding* opened on Broadway in January of 1950. It was reviewed glowingly and went on to win the New York Drama Critics Circle Award for best play. The following year, *Reflections in a Golden Eye* was reissued with a new introduction by Tennessee Williams that sparked serious evaluation of McCullers's work. The collection *The Ballad of the Sad Café: The Novels and Stories of Carson McCullers* was also published. The sale of film rights for *The Member of the Wedding* in the amount of $75,000 brought the McCullerses financial security. In 1952 they traveled in Europe and bought a house in Bachvillers, France, outside of Paris.

Final Years.

Emotionally unstable and debilitated by alcoholism, Reeves proposed mutual suicide to McCullers on several occasions. While McCullers was visiting the United States in 1953, Reeves killed himself. Reeves's death precipitated McCullers's own personal and professional decline. She was further devastated by her mother's death in 1955. Her play *The Square Root of Wonderful* (1958), which many see as a memorial to her mother, opened on Broadway to poor reviews and closed soon after. In 1961 McCullers's novel *Clock Without Hands*, which had taken her nearly a decade to complete, was published to poor reviews that compared it unfavorably with her best work from the 1940s. The playwright Edward Albee's stage adaptation of *The Ballad of the Sad Café* was a moderate success in 1962.

That same year, McCullers's already precarious health declined further. After being diagnosed with breast cancer, she had a mastectomy. In 1964 she was hospitalized for a broken elbow and a broken hip. By 1967 her first two novels had been adapted for film. McCullers was working on a stage musical of *The Member of the Wedding* when she suffered a massive brain hemorrhage. After forty-seven days in a coma, from which she never recovered, she died on September 29 in Nyack, New York.

was awarded a Guggenheim Fellowship. In 1944 her father died of a heart attack, and she moved with her mother to Nyack, New York. She remarried Reeves in 1945, following his medical discharge for injuries sustained in World War II. In 1946 she completed work on *The Member of the Wedding*, which was published to critical acclaim. At the urging of the playwright Tennessee Williams, and partly in response to the literary critic Edmund Wilson's claim that the story lacked a dramatic center, McCullers began adapting her new novel for the stage.

When McCullers won her second Guggenheim Fellowship in 1946, she and Reeves moved to Paris. They returned in 1947, as Reeves spiraled into alcoholism and McCullers convalesced from two more strokes that had left her blind in one eye and partially paralyzed. Despondent about her worsening health, McCullers attempted suicide in 1948.

HIGHLIGHTS IN McCULLERS'S LIFE

1917 Carson McCullers is born Lula Carson Smith on February 19 in Columbus, Georgia.

1926–1934 Studies piano and aspires to career as concert pianist.

1930 Changes name to Carson.

1934 Abandons musical aspirations and moves to New York to study writing.

1936 Publishes her first story, "Wunderkind," in *Story* magazine.

1937 Marries Reeves McCullers and moves to North Carolina.

1940 Moves back to New York; publishes first novel, *The Heart Is a Lonely Hunter*.

1941 Publishes second novel, *Reflections in a Golden Eye*; suffers mild stroke.

1942 Divorces Reeves; receives Guggenheim Fellowship.

1943 Publishes *The Ballad of the Sad Café* in *Harper's*.

1944 Father dies; McCullers moves with her mother to Nyack, New York.

1945 Remarries Reeves.

1946 Publishes *The Member of the Wedding*; befriends Tennessee Williams; receives second Guggenheim Fellowship; moves to Paris with Reeves.

1947 Returns to America after strokes leave her partially blind and paralyzed.

1948 Makes suicide attempt.

1950 Successfully stages *The Member of the Wedding* on Broadway; wins New York Drama Critics Circle Award for best play.

1953 Reeves commits suicide.

1955 Mother dies.

1958 *The Square Root of Wonderful* has brief Broadway run.

1961 McCullers publishes last novel, *Clock Without Hands*.

1962–1964 Suffers from multiple health problems.

1964 Publishes *Sweet as a Pickle, Clean as a Pig*, a book of poems for children.

1967 Suffers a stroke on August 15 and goes into coma; dies September 29.

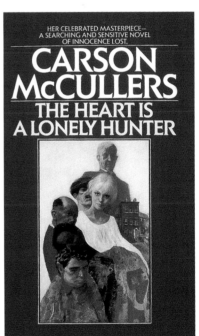

HER CELEBRATED MASTERPIECE—
A SEARCHING AND SENSITIVE NOVEL
OF INNOCENCE LOST.

CARSON
McCULLERS
THE HEART IS
A LONELY HUNTER

The Writer's Work

Carson McCullers is often categorized as a southern writer, but her work employs a variety of settings not exclusively limited to the American South. It may be true that McCullers's pessimistic view of life and the South tempered her fiction, but McCullers's stories are less about twentieth-century southerners than about sensitive human beings. Most of her writings are universal character studies, describing individuals who struggle to overcome personal and social obstacles to love and to achieve a sense of community with others.

McCullers's Characters. McCullers profiled a wide variety of characters in her writing: young and old, rich and poor, white and black, urban and rural. Her characters are varied, but all are emotionally and psychologically complex individuals. McCullers strove to show the people in her stories as united by basic needs and common values that transcend superficial characteristics. *The Heart Is a Lonely Hunter* is a particularly poignant study of individuals from differing backgrounds who fail to appreciate that they move in similar emotional orbits, equal yet distant from one another.

McCullers has been praised for her credible portrayals of both male and African American characters, but her most sensitively developed characters tend to be female adolescents. Mick Kelly in *The Heart Is a Lonely Hunter* and Frankie Addams in *The Member of the Wedding* are her

As in Alexander Brook's 1939 painting *Georgia Jungle* (Carnegie Museum of Art), the characters in McCullers's novels are located in but not limited to the American South. White or black, young or old, rich or poor, they have a universal appeal and share a common bond of "spiritual isolation."

most sensitive depictions of solitary individuals who have outgrown the secure world of childhood innocence but have not yet entered the world of adult experience. Tomboys on the verge of sexual maturity, both Mick and Frankie are characters in states of becoming who are shaped by the disappointments they face. Amelia Evans, the female protagonist of *The Ballad of the Sad Café*, is an adult version of the same character type, vulnerable to a similar fate.

The Theme of Loneliness. In her essay "The Flowering Dream: Notes on Writing," McCullers wrote that "spiritual isolation is the basis of most of my themes." Throughout her writing, characters participate in families, groups, and communities, but they are separated from one another by incommunicable longings. *The Heart Is a Lonely Hunter* depicts a small town where individuals are set apart by unfulfilled aspirations, each limited by his or her age, race, gender, occupation, class, or physical capabilities. In *Reflections in a Golden Eye*, the rigid roles into which people are forced by their society's rules for "normal" sexual identity create unbridgeable emotional gulfs.

In many of McCullers's best works, loneliness and isolation manifest themselves as unrequited love—a longing for affection that is never reciprocated or fails to match the degree to which it is given. Frankie Addams, the teenage protagonist of *The Member of the Wedding*, attempts to force herself into a relationship as an equal with the brother and sister-in-law whom she regards as her soul mates, and she is devastated when they reject her. In *The Ballad of the Sad Café*, which features a similar three-character relationship, McCullers suggests that disproportionate affection between lover and loved one is inevitable.

McCullers and the Grotesque. McCullers's frequent use of grotesque characters and imagery is an outgrowth of the theme of spiritual and emotional alienation. In "The Flowering Dream" she explains, "Love, and love of a person who is incapable of returning and receiving it, is at the heart of my selection of grotesque figures to write about— people whose physical incapacity is a symbol of their spiritual incapacity to love or receive love—their spiritual isolation." The most famous of McCullers's grotesques, Lymon Willis in *The Ballad of the Sad Café*, is a homeless dwarf whose physical difference is an outward sign of the misplaced and unreciprocated affections of the characters with whom he is involved in a love triangle.

McCullers's female adolescents were especially poignant. Having outgrown childhood innocence, they yet lack adult insight and appear as vulnerable and solitary as the child in Simon Dinnerstein's 1977 portrait *The Birthday Dress.*

Michael Dunn and Colleen Dewhurst in a scene from Edward Albee's 1962 adaptation of *The Ballad of the Sad Café* (1943). Focus is on unrequited love as a universal affliction. McCullers would later refer to loneliness as "an American malady."

The grotesque manifests itself in a variety of forms in McCullers's writing. For John Singer in *The Heart Is a Lonely Hunter*, it is in the form of muteness, a physical affliction that prevents him from communicating meaningfully with the people around him. A more intense form of the physical grotesque can be found in *Reflections in a Golden Eye*, in which Alison Langdon, grieving inconsolably for her dead child, mutilates herself. Sometimes, McCullers's grotesquerie is more subtle and self-imposed. Teenage Mick Kelly in *The Heart Is a Lonely Hunter* and Frankie Addams in *The Member of the Wedding* are both tall for their ages and self-conscious of their bodies. Frankie worries that she might fit in with the freak show at a traveling carnival.

McCullers and Violence.
Violence plays a key role in McCullers's fiction. Though it usually serves as a story's climax, it is almost always foreshadowed in events building up to it.

The stylized wrestling match between Amelia Evans and Marvin Macy is a natural outcome to the emotional sparring that has defined their relationship in *The Ballad of the Sad Café*.

The Heart Is a Lonely Hunter features several characters who resort to violence when they are unable to articulate adequately their feelings to others: Bubber Kelly shoots a little girl in a warped expression of emotion toward her, and Jake Blount is unable to put his thoughts into coherent form and resorts to beating his fists against a wall. Both Kelly and Blount anticipate the suicide of John Singer, the mute who has no way to sufficiently express his grief when he learns of the death of his most beloved friend. In *Reflections in a Golden Eye*, the misery of people trapped in unfulfilling situations dictated by constraining social norms breaks out in violence—self-mutilation and brutality against animals—that presages the killing of a harmless character at the story's end.

BIBLIOGRAPHY

Bloom, Harold, ed. *Carson McCullers*. New York: Chelsea House, 1986.

Carr, Virginia Spencer. *The Lonely Hunter: A Biography of Carson McCullers*. New York: Doubleday, 1975.

_____. *Understanding Carson McCullers*. Columbia: University of South Carolina Press, 1990.

Clark, Beverly Lyon, and Melvin J. Friedman, eds. *Critical Essays on Carson McCullers*. New York: G. K. Hall, 1996.

Cook, Richard. *Carson McCullers*. New York: Frederick Ungar, 1972.

Edmonds, Dale. *Carson McCullers*. Austin, Tex.: Steck-Vaughn, 1969.

Evans, Oliver. *The Ballad of Carson McCullers*. New York: Coward-McCann, 1966.

Kiernan, Robert F. *Katherine Anne Porter and Carson McCullers: A Reference Guide*. Boston: G. K. Hall, 1976.

McDowell, Margaret B. *Carson McCullers*. New York: Twayne Publishers, 1980.

Westling, Louise. *Sacred Groves and Ravaged Gardens: The Fiction of Eudora Welty, Carson McCullers, and Flannery O'Connor*. Athens: University of Georgia Press, 1985.

FILMS BASED ON McCULLERS'S STORIES

1953 *The Member of the Wedding*

1967 *Reflections in a Golden Eye*

1968 *The Heart Is a Lonely Hunter*

1982 *The Member of the Wedding* (TV)

1992 *The Ballad of the Sad Café*

1996 *Member of the Wedding*

LONG FICTION

1940 The Heart Is a Lonely Hunter
1941 Reflections in a Golden Eye
1946 The Member of the Wedding
1961 Clock Without Hands

PLAYS

1951 The Member of the Wedding: A Play
1958 The Square Root of Wonderful

POETRY

1964 Sweet as a Pickle, Clean as a Pig

SHORT FICTION

1951 The Ballad of the Sad Café: The Novels and Stories of Carson McCullers
1952 The Ballad of the Sad Café and Collected Short Stories
1971 The Mortgaged Heart
1987 Collected Stories of Carson McCullers

NONFICTION

1999 Illumination and Night Glare: The Unfinished Autobiography of Carson McCullers

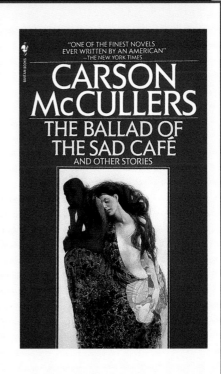

Reader's Guide to Major Works

THE BALLAD OF THE SAD CAFÉ

Genre: Novella
Subgenre: Grotesque fable
Published: 1951
Time period: 1930s
Setting: Southern United States

Themes and Issues. Loneliness takes many forms in Carson McCullers's fiction, the most problematic of which is unrequited love. In *The Ballad of the Sad Café*, McCullers suggests the rarity of relationships that are mutually satisfactory to both the lover and the beloved. More often, the lover expresses intense feelings of affection toward a person who is inappropriate for, or resentful of, such emotion.

The story concerns a love triangle involving three strange, mismatched characters. The surprising shift of alliances occurring at the tale's climax is consistent with the story's themes: that feelings of love are often misplaced and that betrayal is an inevitable risk of any romance.

The Plot. Amelia Evans runs the local feed store and distillery. She has been proud, self-reliant, and aloof since the dissolution of her disastrous ten-day marriage to Marvin Macy when she was nineteen. After she rejected Marvin's attempts to consummate their marriage, he turned to crime and was imprisoned. Her rugged, businesslike manner has made her a rich woman, but she keeps her wealth entirely to herself.

Amelia changes with the arrival of Lymon Willis, a homeless dwarf claiming to be her distant relative. She takes him in and lavishes him with affection, noticeably softening under his influence and becoming more sociable toward the townspeople. She turns her store into a café

In the 1992 film version of *The Ballad of the Sad Café,* Vanessa Redgrave, seen here with Keith Carradine, plays Amelia Evans, one of the strongest of McCullers's fictional women.

that becomes the community's center and a place where Lymon can fit in naturally with his adopted society.

Two years after Amelia's transformation, the town's idyllic peace is threatened by the return of Marvin Macy, who has just been released from prison. Macy's presence aggravates Amelia, but Lymon—whom Marvin despises—unaccountably admires and emulates him.

Events climax with a brawl between Amelia and Marvin, formally staged before the townspeople in the café. Amelia has physically overwhelmed Marvin and is preparing to humiliate him again, when Lymon emerges from the crowd and jumps on her back. The distraction allows Marvin to beat Amelia. The story ends with both Marvin and Lymon disappearing from town concurrently, possibly together, and with Amelia closing down the café and retreating alone inside her store.

SOME INSPIRATIONS BEHIND McCULLERS'S WORK

Carson McCullers has acknowledged the early influence of writers as diverse as the late-nineteenth-century Russian dramatist Anton Chekhov, the mid-nineteenth-century Russian novelist Fyodor Dostoevski, and the early-twentieth-century playwright Eugene O'Neill. The fiction of William Faulkner and Isak Dinesen, on which she wrote perceptive essays, is thought to have contributed to the gothic darkness and grotesque elements in some of her work.

The most obvious inspiration for McCullers's work, however, is her own life. The suburban southern towns of *The Heart Is a Lonely Hunter*, *The Member of the Wedding*, and even *Clock Without Hands* are not unlike her hometown of Columbus, Georgia. It would be unfair to suggest that Frankie Addams and Mick Kelly are simply translations of McCullers's own personality to the printed page, yet both characters resemble McCullers at that age, in their physical attributes and their isolation from peers.

When living in New York, McCullers joined a literary circle that included Richard Wright and W. H. Auden. Here she hosts a dinner given in honor of the Danish author Isak Dinesen, seen sipping champagne, and attended by the actress Marilyn Monroe.

McCullers's father, a jeweler, is the likely inspiration for Mick's watch-repairing dad, and Mick resembles McCullers herself in her eventual abandonment of her musical aspirations.

Some critics suggest that the tortured marital relationships in *Reflections in a Golden Eye* reflect Carson and Reeves McCullers's own marital discord. It is assumed that the army base where the story is set is modeled on Fort Benning, Georgia, where Mary Tucker's husband was stationed. The story itself was supposedly suggested by a story that Reeves told McCullers of a peeping tom soldier.

Analysis. Narrated as a folksy tale with comic overtones, *The Ballad of the Sad Café* marks a departure from McCullers's usual realistic treatments of human love and loss. Her intentionally grotesque characters have a larger-than-life stature that seems appropriate for this allegorical tale. The characters are more symbolically than realistically rendered people, and they help bring the story's reflections on the tribulations of love into sharp focus.

Amelia Evans is the strongest female in McCullers's fiction. Her character is both a celebration of nonconformity and a warning to those who deviate from convention. The three characters—Amelia, Lymon Willis, and Marvin Macy—are often viewed as different aspects of the human condition whose coexistence must inevitably end in self-destruction. Their triangular relationship has been interpreted as a metaphor for the hazards of selfless or unconventional love. One theme that emerges clearly is how Amelia's short-lived, seemingly reciprocated love for Lymon improves her character by allowing her to open herself to greater communion with her society.

SOURCES FOR FURTHER STUDY

Boyle, Kay. "I Wish I Had Written *The Ballad of the Sad Café* by Carson McCullers." In *I Wish I'd Written That: Selections Chosen by Favorite American Authors*, edited by Eugene J. Woods. New York: McGraw-Hill, 1946.

Chamlee, Kenneth D. "Cafés and Community in Three McCullers Novels." *Studies in American Fiction* 18 (Autumn 1990): 233–240.

McNally, John. "The Introspective Narrator in *The Ballad of the Sad Café.*" *South Atlantic Bulletin* 38 (November 1973): 40–44.

Paulson, Suzanne Morrow. "*The Ballad of the Sad Café*: A Song Half-Sung, Misogyny, and 'Ganging Up.'" In *Critical Essays on Carson McCullers*, edited by Beverly Lyon Clark and Melvin J. Friedman. New York: G. K. Hall, 1996.

THE HEART IS A LONELY HUNTER

Genre: Novel
Subgenre: Multiple character study
Published: Boston, 1940
Time period: 1930s
Setting: Southern United States

Themes and Issues. McCullers's first novel is her most sustained exploration of a dominant theme in her fiction—what she referred to in her 1949 essay "Loneliness: An American Malady" as each individual's need "to belong to something larger and more powerful than the weak, lonely self." Focusing on the intersecting lives of people in a small southern town, the novel shows how individuals are thwarted in their efforts to communicate and connect with others by their diverse backgrounds, different ethnicities, and shifting social conditions. The story's title is doubly allusive: The heart is a lonely hunter not only because it undertakes its quest for spiritual communion in solitude but also because, as McCullers demonstrates through the lives of the main characters, that quest is as likely to end in heartbreak and disappointment as in fulfillment.

The Plot. Set in an unnamed southern town at the end of the Great Depression of the 1930s, the novel follows the lives of five main characters as they interact in a number of different situations and settings over a period of several years. The novel's spiritual center is John Singer, a deaf-mute jewelry engraver who is devoted to Spiros Antonapolous, another deaf-mute with whom he rooms. The two men are a study of contrasts: Singer is a fastidious and gentle man whose bearing and manner show signs of intellect and refinement. Antonapolous, a candy maker, is slovenly and self-centered, qualities that are apparently symptoms of a mental deficiency and that lead to his institutionalization.

When Singer moves to smaller lodgings, he meets Mick Kelly, the spirited and independent thirteen-year-old daughter of the owners in whose house he boards. Mick spends most of her time supervising her two younger brothers and is anxious to cross the threshold of adulthood. She loves music, which she seems to understand intuitively, but is frustrated by her inability to master its formal principles. Singer allows her to use the radio in his room.

Mick's relationship with Singer is similar to that of other locals who interact with him in the course of his daily routines: Biff Brannon, who owns the cafe where Singer takes his meals and who struggles to come to terms with his impotence and his wife's death; Jake Blount, a loud and dissipated carnival worker who espouses convoluted radical ideals; and Dr. Benedict Mady Copeland, a proud physician whose marxist beliefs have estranged him from his family and fellow African Americans. Each of these characters uses the kindly but uncommunicative Singer as a spiritual sounding board for their hopes and dreams. The background and personality that each imagines for Singer entirely reflects his or her own beliefs and desires.

The tenuousness of Singer's relationships is revealed when Singer, bereft over his discovery that Antonapolous has died in the asylum, commits suicide. In Singer's absence, the lives of those who were drawn to him seem to fall apart. Biff withdraws socially and cultivates the feminine side of his personality. Jake is involved in a riot at work and must flee town. Dr. Copeland, sick with tuberculosis and broken over the news that his son has been permanently crippled in prison, is taken in by his family. Mick, whose family has endured a number of setbacks and deprivations over the course of the novel, takes a job at the local dime store, forsaking her musical ambitions but still dreaming of owning a piano she will probably never be able to afford.

Analysis. In *The Heart Is a Lonely Hunter*, as in most of her long fiction, McCullers weaves individual character studies into a complex narrative only occasionally leavened by dramatic incidents. The collection of moments from the characters' lives creates a vivid por-

trait of small-town southern life, even though the landscape of the novel is mostly internal. By alternating among multiple viewpoints, she shows loneliness to be a universal affliction ignoring boundaries of race, gender, and age. The narrative's panoramic style contributes to the poignancy of the novel's emotional core, as characters repeatedly interact and regroup, unaware that they all share the same inarticulate need.

The Heart Is a Lonely Hunter typifies McCullers's use of the grotesque with characters whose physical afflictions are outward signs of spiritual or emotional deformity. Key among them is Singer, whom the various characters make into "a home-made God," and whose muteness thus describes not only the inexpressible longings in his own heart but also the unresponsiveness of the universe to human need. Violent incidents in the novel are depicted as the inevitable outcome of emotions

McCullers's first novel, *The Heart Is a Lonely Hunter* (1940) won critical acclaim and quickly launched her career. Author Richard Wright hailed it for its sensitive portrayal of African Americans.

so intense that they cannot be put into coherent or rational forms. This moving and sympathetic novel was widely acclaimed upon its publication and was singled out by author Richard Wright for its humane depiction of African Americans. Its success launched McCullers's career.

SOURCES FOR FURTHER STUDY

Aldridge, Robert. "Two Planetary Systems." In *The Modern American Novel and the Movies*, edited by Gerald Peary and Roger Shatzkin. New York: Frederick Ungar, 1978.

Kestler, Francis. "Gothic Influence of the Grotesque Characters of the Lonely Hunter." *Pembroke Magazine* 20 (1988): 30–36.

Millichap, Joseph R. "The Realistic Structure of *The Heart Is a Lonely Hunter*." *Twentieth Century Literature* 17 (1971): 11–71.

Taylor, Horace. "*The Heart Is a Lonely Hunter*: A Southern Wasteland." In *Studies in American Literature*, edited by Waldo McNeir and Leo B. Levy. Baton Rouge: Louisiana State University Press, 1960.

THE MEMBER OF THE WEDDING

Genre: Novel
Subgenre: Sentimental coming-of-age story
Published: Boston, 1946
Time period: 1944
Setting: Georgia

Themes and Issues. McCullers's best-known story explores her trademark themes of isolation and loneliness from the viewpoint of an adolescent girl desperate to grow up. Frankie Addams, much like Mick Kelly in *The Heart Is a Lonely Hunter*, is poised between the worlds of childhood and adulthood. Eager to leave the self-centered world of youth, she longs for acceptance into grown-up society—specifically, the company of her brother and his bride-to-be, whom Frankie mistakenly believes will take her with them on their impending honeymoon. This is the beginning of an association McCullers refers to as "the we of me."

Frankie's quest for adult identity is a classic study of the painful transition from childhood innocence to adult experience. Her idea of adult life, reflected in the future that she imagines with her brother and sister-in-law, is naïve and unrealistically romanticized. By the story's end, Frankie realizes that the price of the experience that admits her into adulthood is measured in terms of disappointment and disillusionment.

The Plot. In the summer of her twelfth year, Frankie Addams, a tomboy, is "sick and tired of being Frankie." Her best friend has recently moved away, her adolescent temperament has estranged her from her widowed father, and a recent growth spurt has made her feel awkward and unattractive. She has begun to take an interest in the world around her, but she is rejected by the teenage girls she knows, who believe her too young for them. Frankie spends most of her time with her six-year-old cousin, John Henry, and Berenice, the family cook.

Frankie's overly romantic notions of the world have been fed by letters from her brother Jarvis, in Alaska on military duty. When Jarvis returns home to marry Janice Evans, Frankie determines to run off with the couple on their honeymoon and live the exotic, adventurous life to which she imagines the three of them entitled.

Despite Berenice's gentle warnings that she is setting herself up for disappointment, Frankie begins making preparations that she thinks are essential to the future she has planned. She renames herself "F. Jasmine," a name that she thinks will better complement Janice and Jarvis, and begins saying farewells to her acquaintances. A number of her experiences fail to reveal to Frankie how naïve her expectations are: She brings home an orange satin evening dress completely inappropriate for the wedding. She allows a soldier at the local bar who has mistaken her for an older woman to lure her up to his room, escaping his advances only by knocking him out with a water pitcher.

The next day at the wedding, Frankie embarrasses the family by forcing her way into Jarvis and Janice's car. She has to be physically removed once it is clear that the newlyweds do not want her to accompany them. Frankie returns home in shame, and after a failed effort to run away, resigns herself to an ordinary future.

Analysis. *The Member of the Wedding* features some of McCullers's most memorable and sharply drawn characters and is generally acknowledged as the last of her significant fictions. Although not as consciously allegorical as *The Ballad of the Sad Café*, it similarly explores its main theme through the experiences of three different but interrelated characters.

Critics generally agree that Frankie, John Henry, and Berenice represent human experience at three different stages in life. John Henry, who dies of a childhood illness by the story's end, symbolizes the childhood innocence that is inevitably killed by adult experience. Frankie, the budding adolescent, hovers between childhood innocence and adult experience, too knowing for the former but too unrealistic in her presumptions for the latter. Berenice speaks for the reality of adult experience. While relatively young, she has outlived four husbands, each one more disappointing than the previous. Berenice is left alone at the novel's end when John Henry dies, and Frankie—who now goes by the more conventional name Frances—seeks the company of her peers. As such, she captures the solitude and loneliness that is the curse for so many of McCullers's adult characters.

The Member of the Wedding also features one of McCullers's most sensitive and subtle depictions of sexual identity as an alienating aspect of character. A number of characters in McCullers's fiction express their isolation partly through sexual ambiguity, such as Biff

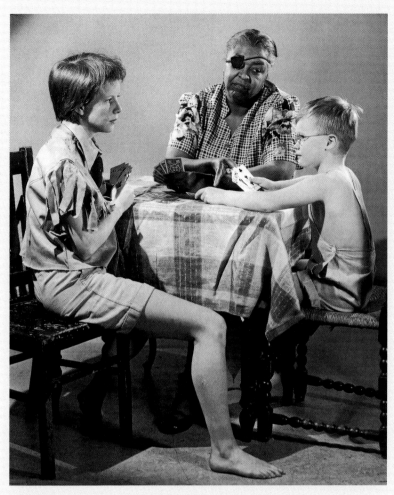

Julie Harris, Ethel Waters, and Brandon de Wilde on Broadway in a scene from *The Member of the Wedding* (1946), a sensitive coming-of-age story that has been adapted for stage, film, and television.

Brannon, whose increasing effeminacy marks his withdrawal from society in *The Heart Is a Lonely Hunter*, and Amelia Evans, the grown-up tomboy of *The Ballad of the Sad Café*.

Frankie's sexual naïveté crystallizes the innocence that will make painful her transition to adulthood. She has only recently stopped sleeping in the same bed as her father, who has begun to notice her physical maturity, and she is hurt by his rejection. Her one experience of sexual experimentation with a boy, indirectly alluded to, has left her disgusted. Her misadventures with the amorous soldier and her childish efforts to include herself in a union that is as much sexual as romantic all express her failure to grasp the sexual dimension of adulthood.

SOURCES FOR FURTHER STUDY

Davis, Thadius M. "Erasing the 'We of Me' and Rewriting the Racial Script: Carson McCullers's Two Member{s} of the Wedding." In *Critical Essays on Carson McCullers*, edited by Beverly Lyon Clark and Melvin J. Friedman. New York: G. K. Hall, 1996.

Westling, Louise. "Carson McCullers's Tomboys." *Southern Humanities Review* 14 (1980): 339–350.

White, Barbara A. "Loss of Self in *The Member of the Wedding*." In *Growing Up Female: Adolescent Girlhood in American Fiction*. Westport, Conn.: Greenwood Press, 1985.

Young, Marguerite. "Metaphysical Fiction." *Kenyon Review* 9 (Winter 1947).

Other Works

CLOCK WITHOUT HANDS (1961). Written over a decade punctuated by her medical problems, Carson McCullers's last work of fiction is her most socially conscious. The contemporary, episodic novel is set in a small Georgia town seething with racist, antebellum attitudes. It studies the South's uneasy acknowledgment of desegregation and civil rights.

The novel's most sympathetic character, J. T. Malone, a druggist, is diagnosed with incurable leukemia. Seeking spiritual salvation, Malone reflects on his life and his relations with other characters in town. Primary among these relationships is Malone's friendship with Fox Clane, an aging and sickly judge who is nostalgic about the old Confederacy and vigorously opposed to racial integregation. His eighteen-year-old grandson, Jester, who lives with him, strongly disagrees with his racial views. Jester befriends and is attracted to Sherman Pew, an eighteen-year-old African American who is likewise an orphan. Jester eventually discovers that Sherman is the son of a man whom Jester's father unsuccessfully defended against charges that he murdered the husband of his white lover. When Judge Fox Clane sentenced Sherman's father to death, Jester's father committed suicide. This revelation severs Jester's ties to his grandfather.

Sherman's similar discovery of Clane's role in his father's death drives him from the Clane house, where he has been serving as the judge's assistant. Sherman moves into an all-white neighborhood, inciting Clane to raise a lynch mob. In a crucial moment, Malone refuses to join the mob, which ultimately bombs Sherman's house, killing him. Jester later finds himself in a position to kill the leader of the lynch mob but resists, deciding instead to follow his father into law and continue his good works. The novel closes on May 17, 1954, the day that the Supreme Court ordered the desegregation of public schools. The enfeebled

A house in Columbus, Georgia, birthplace of Carson McCullers. A town like any number of suburban southern towns, Columbus influenced the author's choice of setting for much of her work.

Reflections in a Golden Eye (1941), McCullers's shocking second novel, is considered an account of the disintegration of her first marriage to the troubled Reeves. Marlon Brando and Elizabeth Taylor starred in the 1967 film.

Clane is powerless to turn the tide of history, and Malone dies indifferent to Clane's efforts.

REFLECTIONS IN A GOLDEN EYE (1941). McCullers's second novel is a virtually plotless character study of six people who are party to the tragic consequences of an extramarital affair. Set on a southern army base, it juxtaposes the rigid conformity and customs of military life with the wildly raging emotions of its characters. It explores in a richly symbolic narrative the destructive potential of sexual insecurity.

Captain Wendell Penderton is trapped in a loveless union with his wife, Leonora. Sexually impotent, and potentially bisexual, he maintains his marriage for appearances only. Leonora makes little effort to conceal her frustration with him or her affair with a neighbor, Major Morris Langdon. Langdon's wife, the neurotic Alison, has been in frail health since mutilating herself after the death of her malformed infant child. Alison strongly suspects her husband's infidelities and confides in Anacleto, an effeminate houseboy who serves as her surrogate child.

The novel's catalyst is Ellgee Williams, a private employed by Penderton to tend Leonora's horse. The sexually inexperienced Williams has an almost instinctive connection with the natural world that both attracts and repulses Penderton. Williams is capable of handling horses, a skill Penderton clearly lacks.

Williams becomes fascinated with Leonora and steals nightly into her room to watch as she sleeps. One night, he is seen by Alison, who assumes the figure to be her husband sneaking into the Penderton house for a liaison. Alison is relentless in her suspicions, even after discovering that it was Williams, and not Langdon, in Leonora's room. She attempts to run away but is stopped by her husband, and she later dies in an institution. Penderton, alerted by Alison, catches Williams in Leonora's room and shoots him, symbolically killing the masculine spirit that Williams represents.

Dedicated to McCullers's lover Annemarie Clarac-Schwarzenbach, *Reflections in a Golden Eye* is considered by many critics an autobiographical work about Carson and Reeves McCullers's growing sexual estrangement. Although Tennessee Williams praised the novel as one of McCullers's strongest works, its frank subject matter was criticized harshly by reviewers.

Resources

Institutions and organizations of interest to students of Carson McCullers include

The Carson McCullers Society. This society was founded in 1997 at the convention of the American Literature Association and is based at the University of West Florida at Pensacola. It is dedicated to furthering scholarly interest in McCullers's life and work, sponsoring papers that contribute to ongoing critical conversation about contemporary issues in McCullers studies at the American Literature Association Conference. (http://www.uwf.edu/english/McCullers/main.htm)

The Carson McCullers Project. This project is a Web-based directory of biographical and bibliographical information on McCullers, with links to other sites of interest to students of McCullers and her writings. (http://www.carson-mccullers.com/)

Teaching Carson McCullers. Sponsored by EducETH, this is a Web-based forum for student and teacher discussion of McCullers's writings. It includes a biography, a time line, a bibliography of McCullers and her work, and capsule synopses of selected titles. It also features a bulletin board for posting queries and commentaries. (http://educeth.ethz.ch/english/readinglist/mccullersc/index.html)

STEFAN DZIEMIANOWICZ

D'Arcy McNickle

BORN: January 18, 1904, St. Ignatius, Montana
DIED: October 18, 1977, Albuquerque, New Mexico
IDENTIFICATION: Mid-twentieth-century Native American novelist, biographer, historian, anthropologist, administrator, and activist.

One of the first Native American novelists, D'Arcy McNickle is also regarded as one of the best. His realistic fiction depicts the hard lives of rural Americans on reservations, farms, and ranches during the Great Depression of the 1930s. His sensitive stories detailing the consequences of Euro-American ethnocentrism neither romanticize nor demonize Native Americans. Although he was successful as a writer, McNickle is equally remembered for his efforts to improve the prospects of Native American peoples through his service in the federal Bureau of Indian Affairs (BIA), his organization of the National Congress of American Indians (NCAI), and his development of the Center for the History of the American Indian at Newberry Library in Chicago.

The Writer's Life

On January 18, 1904, William D'Arcy McNickle was born near St. Ignatius, Montana, on the Flathead Reservation of the Salish and Kootenai people. He was the third child of William McNickle, of Scotch-Irish descent, and Philomene Parenteau, of Canadian Cree and French (métis) ancestry. McNickle's mixed heritage and his school years with his Indian peers later contributed to his lifelong efforts to analyze the nature and consequences of the Indian-European encounter from an American Indian point of view.

Childhood and Youth. McNickle spent his childhood on the Flathead Reservation in the spectacular Big Sky country of western Montana. His parents divorced in April 1913.

McNickle attended the St. Ignatius Mission School, run by Jesuits and the Sisters of Providence, and later the Salem Indian Training School, known as Chemawa, in Salem, Oregon. He attended the University of Montana, but at the end of his senior year, he lacked sufficient units to graduate. A brief period of travel in England and France furthered his taste for writing, travel, and culture, but finances forced his early return to the United States.

The Once and Future Writer. At the University of Montana, McNickle wrote poetry, studied literature, and worked on the college literary magazine. The experience he gained with various publishers allowed him in 1929 to become a publisher's assistant at the *National Cyclopedia*

Of mixed heritage, McNickle was born in Montana on the Flathead Reservation of the Salish and Kootenai people in 1904. Shown here is a 1910 photograph of a Salish Indian camp on the Jocko River.

One of the earliest and best Native American novelists, McNickle celebrated his culture, especially its song and storytelling. Native American rites and rituals, such as this Flathead Reservation dance, figured prominently in his writing.

of American Biography in New York City. The position enabled him to eke out a living for himself and his first wife, Joran Birkeland, during the Great Depression. In New York, McNickle read omnivorously at the New York Public Library.

During this time, McNickle also began work on his first novel, which was later published as *The Surrounded* (1936) after being rejected by a number of publishers and revised extensively. In the same year he moved from a job with the Federal Writers' Project to the Bureau of Indian Affairs (BIA), where he worked with John Collier, an innovative reformer who sought to preserve tribal identities and Indian ownership of lands and other property.

Indian Affairs. McNickle spent sixteen years with the BIA. His work there and his contacts with such anthropologists as William Gates helped him to develop his views on cultural relativity, especially the idea that the near impossibility of effective cross-cultural communication lay at the heart of the conflict between American Indians and Euro-Americans. This idea became a central theme throughout

McNickle's writing. Despite his wholehearted involvement with the BIA and the nearly nonexistent sales of *The Surrounded*, McNickle was always writing. He produced professional papers on Indian life and affairs, book reviews, short fiction, and novels, including *Runner in the Sun: A Story of Indian Maize* (1954) and *Wind from an Enemy Sky* (1978).

In 1944 McNickle organized the National Congress of American Indians (NCAI), an organization uniting Indians on a national level. After leaving the BIA in 1952, he worked on numerous projects associated with the NCAI, including a series of community development projects in Crownpoint, New Mexico.

Marriage and Domestic Life. In November 1926, McNickle had married the first of his three wives, Joran Birkeland, with whom he had one child, Antoinette (Toni). However, the couple separated in 1936 and divorced two years later. In 1939 McNickle married Roma Kauffman, a writer and editor for the United States Office of Education. Their daughter, Kathleen, was born in 1941. McNickle divorced Roma in 1967 and married his third

A self-taught cultural anthropologist, McNickle also wrote ethnohistories. Though his literary work received little attention in his lifetime, his scholarly study of Native American culture earned him recognition. Here, in a photograph taken in the 1930s, the time frame of most of his fiction, Salish women prepare a meal.

wife, Viola Pfrommer, two years later. Viola was a sociologist who had worked as a health educator at Crownpoint from 1953 to 1960. By the time of her marriage to McNickle, she had already developed early symptoms of Alzheimer's disease, and she died a few months before he did in 1977.

Scholarship and Recognition. A self-taught cultural anthropologist, McNickle earned public and scholarly recognition for his tireless advocacy for Native Americans as a BIA administrator from 1936 to 1952, for his scholarly contributions to Native American education, and for his significant literary output

of nonfiction, novels, articles, and short stories, many of which were published posthumously.

McNickle was awarded an honorary doctorate from the University of Colorado in 1966, the same year in which he accepted an appointment as the founding chair of the anthropology department at the University of Saskatchewan's new Regina campus. From 1972 until his death on October 18, 1977, McNickle served as founding program director at the Center for the History of the American Indian at the Newberry Library, which was renamed in his honor as the D'Arcy McNickle Center for the History of the American Indian.

HIGHLIGHTS IN McNICKLE'S LIFE

1904   William D'Arcy McNickle is born on January 18 on the Flathead and Kootenai Reservation near St. Ignatius, Montana.

1913   His parents divorce; McNickle enrolls at the Salem Indian Training School, Chemawa, in Salem, Oregon.

1921   Graduates from high school in Missoula, Montana; enrolls at the University of Montana in Missoula.

1925   Sails for England; intends to matriculate at Oxford University but is denied admission.

1926   Returns to New York; marries Joran Birkeland.

1929   Studies history at Columbia University; completes handwritten draft of his first novel, "The Hungry Generations," which is rejected by Harcourt, Brace.

1933   First daughter, Antoinette, is born; McNickle forms association with William Gates, who introduces him to the idea of cultural relativity.

1935   Joins the Federal Writers' Project.

1936   Publishes *The Surrounded*; transfers to the Bureau of Indian Affairs (BIA).

1938   Divorces his first wife, Joran.

1939   Marries Roma Kauffman.

1941   Second daughter, Kathleen, is born.

1944   McNickle helps found the National Congress of American Indians.

1952   Resigns from the BIA.

1953   Establishes a health education and community development project among the Navajos at Crownpoint, New Mexico.

1954   Publishes *Runner in the Sun*.

1959   Coauthors (with Harold Fey) *Indians and Other Americans: Two Ways of Life Meet*.

1965   Publishes the first of many reviews of Indian material for *The Nation*.

1966   Receives honorary doctorate from University of Colorado; accepts appointment as founding chair of the anthropology department at the University of Saskatchewan.

1967   Divorces Roma Kauffman.

1969   Marries Viola Pfrommer.

1971   Builds home in Albuquerque, New Mexico; publishes *Indian Man: A Biography of Oliver La Farge*.

1972   Is appointed founding director for the Center for the History of the American Indian at the Newberry Library in Chicago (later renamed in his honor).

1973   Revises his earlier *Indian Tribes of the United States* as *Native American Tribalism: Indian Survivals and Renewals*.

1977   His third wife, Viola, dies; McNickle dies of heart attack on October 18 in Albuquerque, New Mexico.

1978   *Wind from an Enemy Sky* is published posthumously.

1992   *The Hawk Is Hungry and Other Stories* is published posthumously.

D'Arcy McNickle published many works in a variety of genres, including three novels, a biography, three ethnohistories, and numerous articles and book reviews. In addition, a selection of over forty of McNickle's short stories was edited and published in 1992. Although McNickle's literary significance went largely unacknowledged in his lifetime, McNickle is now recognized as one of the originators of modern Native American literature and ethnohistory. He is considered a writer of power and perceptiveness whose melding of boyhood experiences, tribal myth, and scholarly study of Native American cultures makes his work both engaging and true.

Issues in McNickle's Fiction. In both his fiction and his nonfiction, McNickle explored the culture conflicts between American Indians and Euro-Americans. In *The Surrounded* and *Wind from an Enemy Sky*, McNickle attacks federal policies and legislation, particularly the General Allotment Act (or Dawes Severalty Act) of 1887, which encouraged the assimilation, if not the extermination, of Native American culture by imposing a system of individual land ownership on many Indian tribes and opening the remaining land to white settlement.

Also central to McNickle's fiction is the power and function of Native American song, storytelling, and traditional celebratory behaviors studied "from both sides," as John Purdy puts it, as a "Salish/Cree man seeking knowledge . . . in voluntary isolation from his family and their land." Furthermore, in *Runner in the Sun*, McNickle celebrates the important contributions of Native Americans to the agriculture and prosperity of postcontact world cultures.

At the same time, he laments the wanton destructiveness of the European invaders, who

McNickle was a tireless advocate of Native Americans. An administrator with the Bureau of Indian Affairs for sixteen years, he especially opposed the unfair land distribution of the General Allotment Act of 1887. Juane Quick-to-See-Smith's 1992 painting *Trade (Gifts for Trading Land with White People)* explains why.

advanced over the land with little capacity for anything but exploitation. McNickle felt that the world might have benefited from the contact if European settlers had only "adopted and carried away with them the respect for peaceful living which characterized the first Americans." McNickle the anthropologist and ethnologist is solidly and compellingly present in the work of McNickle the fiction writer.

People in McNickle's Fiction.

McNickle's three novels feature a number of Native American men and women, young and old, who attempt in various ways to understand, resist, accommodate to, or assimilate with the aftermath of Euro-American conquest. McNickle's characters are believable, sympathetic, and unique individuals, not the romanticized or demonized Indians of popular fiction written by Euro-Americans.

McNickle created such memorable figures as Archilde Leon, the son of the Spaniard Max Leon and Catherine Le Loup, the Salish Indian daughter of Running Wolf, in *The Surrounded*. In *Wind from an Enemy Sky*, Henry Jim, and Two Sleeps are among the elders and leaders of the Little Elk band, who argue that "the white man makes us forget our holy places. He makes us small." Their white counterparts in the story are A. T. Rafferty, the Indian agent; Adam Pell, the dreamy industrialist who collects artifacts; and Stephen Welles, the old missionary who seeks to "civilize the savages" by destroying their culture and its artifacts. These men—all good people in their own eyes and in those of their subcultures—are not only fully realized individuals but also types who represent the conflicting cultures. Inevitably, each is doomed by the forces of misunderstanding and anger that stem from cultural differences, the tragic wrongheadedness of federal policy,

Pigeon's Egg Head, Going to and Returning from Washington (Smithsonian American Art Museum) by George Catlin demonstrates the superficial value of the cultural exchange that took place between the Native Americans and Europeans. McNickle especially lamented the fact that the Euro-Americans, who could have learned from Native Americans, only exploited them.

and decades of white oppression of Native American peoples.

McNickle's young-adult novel *Runner in the Sun* is set in the pre-Hispanic area now known as the American Southwest. Salt, the protagonist, is a young boy who resists the dark forces of evil in his village and goes on a long heroic journey to gather knowledge of other peoples as well as new seed corn, and he returns to restore vigor to his people.

The Theme of Cultural Ethnocentrism.

McNickle explores in his fiction the conflicts that result when two peoples with fundamentally different worldviews—Native Americans and Europeans and Euro-Americans—come into contact with each other. He portrays Europeans as aggressive, exploitative, and ra-

Storytelling is an art, and Velino Shije Herrera's painting *Story Teller* (Smithsonian American Art Museum, Washington, D. C.), ca. 1925–1935, conveys the respect it is shown in Native American culture. In recent years, McNickle, who died in 1977, is finally receiving the appreciation he too deserves.

pacious, coming into the New World with the idea of owning the land, of exploiting its natural resources and native people and animals, and of imposing their spirituality and cultural values upon the Native Americans. The Native Americans are baffled by the behavior of these invaders and ultimately react with rage at the continuing destruction of their way of life. The result in both *The Surrounded* and *Wind from an Enemy Sky* is as tragic and instructive as Greek or Shakespearean tragedy and emerges in the actions of characters who are fully realized and sympathetic individuals.

McNickle's Literary Legacy. Now considered one of the founders of Native American fiction, McNickle earned recognition for the mythic qualities of his fiction, the thematic complexity of his narratives, and the depth and fullness of his characterizations. Both his first and last novels were written during the 1930s. *Wind from an Enemy Sky*, finally published in 1978, underwent revision for over forty years, as McNickle pursued his varied careers as administrator, anthropologist, and advocate.

With the reprinting of his first two novels by the University of New Mexico and the publication of a short fiction collection, McNickle's work has received increased scholarly attention and has attracted a wider and more appreciative readership.

BIBLIOGRAPHY

Ortiz, Alfonso. "Darcy McNickle (1904–1977): Across the River and Up the Hill, a Personal Remembrance." *American Indian* 4, no. 4 (April 1978): 12–16.

Parker, Dorothy R. *Singing an Indian Song: A Biography of D'Arcy McNickle*. Lincoln: University of Nebraska Press, 1992.

Purdy, John Lloyd, ed. *The Legacy of D'Arcy McNickle: Writer, Historian, Activist*. Norman: University of Oklahoma Press, 1996.

———. *Word Ways: The Novels of D'Arcy McNickle*. Tucson: University of Arizona Press, 1990.

Ruppert, James. *D'Arcy McNickle*. Boise, Idaho: Boise State University Press, 1988.

Schuman, R. Baird. "McNickle, Darcy." In *Identities and Issues in Literature*, edited by David Peck. Vol. 2. Pasadena, Calif.: Salem Press, 1997.

Reader's Guide to Major Works

RUNNER IN THE SUN: A STORY OF INDIAN MAIZE

Genre: Novel
Subgenre: Young-adult fiction
Published: Albuquerque, New Mexico, 1954
Time period: Before the sixteenth century
Setting: Southwestern United States; Mexico.

Themes and Issues. Based on extensive research into the work of such ethnographers as Elsie Clews Parsons and Adolf Bandelier, *Runner in the Sun* is a novel rich in information about Native American peoples at an early period in history.

The Plot. The young hero, Salt, goes on a long journey to find new corn seed for his tribe. Along the way he encounters challenges that test and train him, and he learns about different peoples and their cultures. He returns with the corn seed and a bride from one of the distant cultures, bringing newness both to his people and to their principal food staple. Salt enacts the archetypal journey of the hero who returns to his native village to lead, change, and build it anew. McNickle grounds Salt's adventures in a power struggle between good and evil in the form of two rival clans. Salt learns and reinforces the strengths of tribalism and warns against excesses of power and powerlessness that threaten to destroy the Native American peoples.

Analysis. Although it was written for young-adult readers, *Runner in the Sun* is of interest to anyone seeking to understand the power of origin myths in native cultures. Part of the novel's strength lies in McNickle's cogent use of Native American oral tradition, in which the higher goal is not to amuse but to educate. The story is presented in a Native American fashion, as an oral tale rather than a written story. The sentences are short; the point of view is omniscient, as in traditional storytelling; and the story closes with a summary of the consequences, an ending typical of the oral tradition.

SOURCES FOR FURTHER STUDY

Parker, Dorothy R. *Singing an Indian Song: A Biography of D'Arcy McNickle.* Lincoln: University of Nebraska Press, 1992.

Purdy, John Lloyd. *Word Ways: The Novels of D'Arcy McNickle.* Tucson: University of Arizona Press, 1990.

The harsh terrain of the Southwest, as revealed in this photograph of Monument Valley, Arizona, could easily be the setting of *Runner in the Sun: A Story of Indian Maize,* McNickle's young-adult novel.

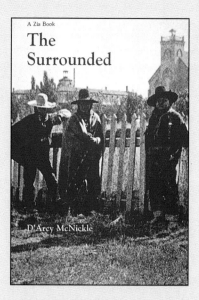

A Zia Book

The Surrounded

D'Arcy McNickle

THE SURROUNDED

Genre: Novel
Subgenre: Historical tragedy
Published: New York, 1936
Time period: Late nineteenth to early twentieth century
Setting: Western Montana

Themes and Issues. The central theme of this novel is the near impossibility of American Indian assimilation, as political and social policy and as individual practice. The so-called civilizing institutions of Euro-American society—its religion, government, and economy—stand always in opposition to the culture of the American Indian. Related to this dichotomy are the continuing consequences of ethnocentrism exhibited by the representatives of each of these institutions at every level of contact.

Another theme involves issues of identity and examines the question posed by Archilde's Hispanic father: "What kind of Indian are you?" It is a question central to both plot and theme and is embodied in the character of Archilde Leon, a man who is caught between the two worlds of conquered and conqueror, of the "American" and the "Indian."

Family relationships play an important role in *The Surrounded*. The conflicts of the father with his seven sons and the conflicts among brothers become metaphors for the wider conflicts among races and social groups that lead to confusion, pain, dread, and emptiness. The novel also celebrates the vanishing beauty of the valley and the threatened American Indian way of life.

The Plot. Archilde Leon—a mixed-blood Indian, the son of a Spanish cattleman father, Max Leon, and a Salish mother, Catherine—returns from the city to visit his father's ranch on the Flathead Indian Reservation in Montana. He becomes entangled in the clash between the Euro-American culture of the white settlers and the traditional culture of the Native Americans. Archilde witnesses the destructive effects of reservation life on his people and endures the deep-seated anger that Max directs toward his seven sons.

Archilde, knowing that work is a central value in Max's life, works hard on the farm to earn the old man's gradual respect, the only one of seven sons to do so. Archilde tries to understand the nature of his parents' estrangement and the reason why his mother and father live separately in houses next to each other. He also becomes reacquainted with the traditional life of the tribe and its ceremonies, songs, and stories.

On a fall hunt deep in the mountains, Louis, one of Archilde's brothers who had been changed by the "school of the Fathers," is shot and killed by the game warden. Catherine, their mother, then kills the game warden with a hatchet. Archilde hides the game warden's body but takes Louis's body back home to be buried. Sheriff Quigley hunts for the warden's body and later for the killer, suspecting Archilde and pursuing him to the novel's surprising and tragic conclusion.

Analysis. McNickle created a parallel structure to highlight the culture clash between Native American and Euro-American peoples that forms the basis of this novel. There are two communities and two houses in which Archilde's parents live. There are two dances, one at the Farmers' Hall and one a part of the Indian ceremony. The community has two religions and two types of education. Two old men, Modeste and Father Grepilloux, vie for Archilde's soul. The men make two trips into the mountains. Throughout the novel, the bipartite structure enables and enacts the conflicts that lock the characters into various fatal embraces.

SOURCES FOR FURTHER STUDY

Parker, Robert Dale. "Who Shot the Sheriff: Storytelling, Indian Identity, and the Marketplace of Masculinity in D'Arcy McNickle's *The Surrounded.*" *Modern Fiction Studies* 43 (Winter 1997): 898–932.

Ruppert, James. "Textual Perspectives and the Reader in *The Surrounded.*" In *Narrative Chance: Postmodern Discourse on Native American Indian Literatures,* edited by Gerald Vizenor. Albuquerque: University of New Mexico Press, 1989.

McNickle focuses on family, tribal, and ethnic interrelationships. As depicted in LaVerne Nelson Black's 1938 painting *Ceremonial at Black Lake* (Smithsonian American Art Museum), a tribe comes together. In the author's first novel, *The Surrounded* (1936), a family is torn apart.

WIND FROM AN ENEMY SKY
Genre: Novel
Subgenre: Historical tragedy
Published: New York, 1978
Time period: 1930s
Setting: Western Montana

Themes and Issues. As he did in *The Surrounded,* McNickle attacks federal policies, especially the General Allotment Act of 1887 that sought to assimilate or exterminate all Native American cultures. He explores the practical effects of those policies, which included the appropriation and destruction of tribal land and resources. He implicates the government in the kidnappings of Indian children, in their forced removal to Indian boarding schools far from their homes, in the prohibition of Indian language and customs, and in the imposition of European cultural values, especially those of the Christian religion.

The Plot. A long-standing division exists between a traditionalist leader of the Little Elk people, Bull, and his brother, Henry Jim, a "progressive" who has adopted agriculture and built a "white man's house." When the dam built by Adam Pell steals the water, Bull's deep-seated rage and frustration lead his grandson to kill an engineer at the dam, ironically Adam Pell's son.

Pell, it turns out, had years before come into possession of "the sacred Feather Boy bundle," which, ignorantly cast aside in a museum, is destroyed. When the Little Elk people, believing that the Feather

The forced removal of Native American boys to boarding schools far away from home was one of the many injustices of the General Allotment Act of 1887. McNickle himself attended the Salem Indian Training School in Salem, Oregon.

Boy bundle is about to be returned to them, learn the truth, Bull kills Pell and Toby Rafferty, a decent Indian agent. Bull is then killed by an Indian tribal policeman.

SOME INSPIRATIONS BEHIND McNICKLE'S WORK

D'Arcy McNickle was greatly influenced by his early life on the reservation and his early schooling at St. Ignatius Mission School and at Chemawa Indian School. His close relationship with his mother, especially after his parents' divorce, was another important influence on his development. An important element in McNickle's intellectual evolution was his study of literature at the University of Montana, where he was encouraged by a professor to go to England. The months McNickle spent in England and later in France gave him a cosmopolitan view of the world that did not, however, destroy his ability to make use of his Salish Indian cultural roots. Although he did not return to live on the reservation, he saw the literary possibilities of his mixed-blood life there.

Many critics see evidence of the influence of both Ernest Hemingway's and Gertrude Stein's literary styles in McNickle's work. However, McNickle's use of tribal life and culture remains uniquely his own.

Analysis. McNickle's third novel evolved over more than thirty years from a 1944 draft of "The Flight of Feather Boy" to its posthumous publication as *Wind from an Enemy Sky*. Two cultural symbols lie at the heart of the novel: the dam as a symbol of white conquest and containment, destroying both the Little Elk people's holy grounds and diverting water to the white farming community; and the medicine bundle, Feather Boy, a sacred object at the center of the tribe's spiritual and communal life.

The theft and destruction of the Feather Boy bundle by the agents of the Euro-American culture symbolizes the Euro-American oppression of the Native Americans, here the Little Elk people. Adam Pell's dam steals the Little Elks' water. Bull's grandson kills Pell's son, who, in working on the dam, is complicit in its power and function. Pell's recognition and articulation that justice consistently has been denied to the Little Elk people comes too late to save either himself or the Little Elk. All efforts at mediation between the two cultures fail.

SOURCES FOR FURTHER STUDY

Parker, Dorothy R. *Singing an Indian Song: A Biography of D'Arcy McNickle*. Lincoln: University of Nebraska Press, 1992.

Purdy, John Lloyd. *The Legacy of D'Arcy McNickle: Writer, Historian, Activist*. Norman: University of Oklahoma Press, 1996.

Other Works

THE HAWK IS HUNGRY AND OTHER STORIES (1992). These sixteen stories—ten of which were previously unpublished—were written in the years from 1927 to 1935, while D'Arcy McNickle was living in New York City and working on his first novel. Several of the stories were originally part of "The Hungry Generations," the title of an early draft of his later novel *The Surrounded*. They include "Snowfall," "Hard Riding," and "Train Time." The stories are arranged according to three themes, reservation, Montana, and the city, all of which reflect McNickle's concern with a sense of place. McNickle's gritty, realistic stories "Hard Riding" and "Man's Work" compare favorably with those of early-twentieth-century authors, such as Willa Cather, O. E. Rölvaag, and Hamlin Garland, who painted realistic, unsentimental portraits of the Midwest.

In "The Hawk Is Hungry," two sisters face the challenges of farming in the arid, mountainous West. Their rural life is quite different from their romantic dreams. Several other stories in the volume are set in New York City and reflect the lives of young people struggling for success in the big city. "Six Beautiful in Paris" and "In the Alien Corn" are reminiscent of short stories by F. Scott Fitzgerald and Ernest Hemingway and suggest something of McNickle's narrative power. McNickle's stories shed light on the life and concerns of one of the most important twentieth-century American Indian leaders, and they stand as well on their own merit.

NATIVE AMERICAN TRIBALISM: INDIAN SURVIVALS AND RENEWALS (1973). In this book, published for the Institute of Race Relations by Oxford University Press, McNickle surveys the years of "inter-ethnic contact in the New World." He notes especially the efforts of the French and English to colonize the eastern seaboard of America and the resulting displacements of the Native American peoples by purchase, treaty, and conquest. Until the late twentieth century, the ruling assumption by the Euro-American settlers was that Indians were a "vanishing race," doomed to extinction. McNickle's historical survey summarizes official, but ultimately ineffectual, efforts by popes, kings, and statesmen to ensure that no Indian land be occupied by settlers without official permission from the original population.

Although McNickle's tone is dispassionate and scholarly throughout, he reveals the ironies as well as the contemporary consequences of the fight for an equitable ethnic policy. He cites the successful decades-long struggle of the Taos Indians of New Mexico to reclaim their spiritual shrine at Blue Lake on Taos Mountain as an example of the policy of cultural tolerance "which must be the basis of any commitment in support of self-determination."

THEY CAME HERE FIRST: THE EPIC OF THE AMERICAN INDIAN (1949). The first historical survey of American Indian–European relations to be written by a Native American, this book was partly a response to a question asked by a Hopi man about the arrogance of the uninvited Europeans who imposed their own rules and customs on Native Americans. Much of McNickle's work and writing involved his crusade to convince all Americans to address the same question. Both Europeans and Native Americans judged each other by the values and principles of their respective cultures with disastrous consequences—a theme that McNickle addressed in his last, posthumously published novel, *Wind from an Enemy Sky*.

Resources

D'Arcy McNickle's papers, including manuscripts, drafts, and correspondence, were donated in 1983 by McNickle's daughter, Toni, to the Newberry Library in Chicago, Illinois. The Newberry is the home of the D'Arcy McNickle Center for American Indian History, of which McNickle himself was the founding director. Other sources of interest for students of McNickle include the following:

D'Arcy McNickle Center for American Indian History. Originally founded in 1972 at the Newberry Library as the Center for the History of the American Indian and later renamed in McNickle's honor, the center trains scholars, teachers, and tribal historians in a new approach to Indian history by collecting and archiving tribal materials for scholarly study. The center has played a major role in shaping the field of American Indian history. (http://www.newberry.org/nl/mcnickle/darcyhome.html)

D'Arcy McNickle Library. A library at Salish Kootenai College in Pablo, Montana, on the Flathead Reservation where McNickle was raised was dedicated in 1987. (http://skcweb.skc.edu/media/media_ctr_descp.html)

Native American Educational Services. Based in Chicago, this "university without walls" serves elementary, secondary, and adult Native American students with community-based academic programs. (http://naes.indian.com)

THEODORE C. HUMPHREY

Index

Page numbers in **boldface** type indicate article titles. Page numbers in *italic* type indicate illustrations.